RETURN to the FOLD

John M. Collins ■ Don Garwood ■ Thay Yang

McGraw-Hill, Inc.

New York St. Louis San Francisco Auckland Bogotá
Caracas Lisbon London Madrid Mexico Milan Montreal
New Delhi Paris San Juan Singapore Sydney Tokyo Toronto

RETURN TO THE FOLD

1 2 3 4 5 6 7 8 9 0 SEM SEM 9 0 9 8 7 6 5

ISBN 0-07-011853-1

Editor: Todd Bull
Folding Illustrations: Thay Yang
Cover Design and Graphic Design: David M. Daly
Printer/Binder: Quebecor Printing Semline, Inc.

Introduction

Wonderous and thrilling. From the lowly aphid to the top secret project Aurora, the spectacle of flight is amazing. Isn't it miraculous that simple folding can emulate a feat that took millions of years to evolve? How do paper airplanes fly? It is exhiliarating watching a paper glider on it's maiden flight. You've mananged to turn one of the most basic and widely available building blocks of civilization into a gliding machine. This handmade machine easily accomplishes an act fascinating to humans for milenia: flight. Your spirit soars with the plane as it performs its dance on the air. You may almost sense yourself onboard gracefully floating or perhaps careening at break-neck speed through the air.

The variety of possible shapes is also astounding. The ordinary 8 1/2 x 11 inch sheet of paper (lettersize) has yet to be exhausted; even though it's been available in this country for about 250 years!

This book is a collaboration between three people who really enjoy (read that obsess about) creating and flying paper airplanes. New paper glider designs, new folding techniques, as well as some novel launching and flying techniques are all explained in easy details. All you need to start is a piece of paper.

There are several ways to use this book. But foremost is to let yourself fantasize. You are the creator of an elegant paper form: its story and meaning, too. We have given some of the gliders names, but feel free to rename as suits you. Secondly, enjoy the folding. Be aware of the new shapes as they emerge. Enjoy some of the folding tricks (moves) that magically produce a whole new or unexpected shape. And finally, experience your growing power and control over flight. We explain enough of flight mechanics so you can develope mastery based on understanding. Its a good feeling, knowing how to achieve your desired flight.

CONTENTS

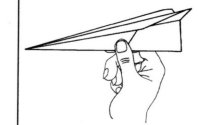

Why Paper Gliders?

DON GARWOOD

For a few wonderful years I lived in a small cabin on the Pacific coast near Mendocino. One winter the rains just would not stop. Everyday I woke up to the sound of rainfall on the roof. Rain and more rain. And the wind! The rain came at you horizontally! So we stayed indoors most days, and I was going bananas with cabin fever.

One day in desperation I braved the stormy wet in order to visit the kite shop in Mendocino. Don't ask me why. The conditions were far from favorable to kite flying. I guess I was just over the edge and needed something different to do. The shop had a paper glider book for sale, Hans Bergan's The Lingore Paper Airplane Folding Manual. Scanning the book I realized I didn't know paper airplanes could be so intriguing. I purchased a copy, and protecting it from the rain inside my rain coat, took it home.

That book saved my sanity from the endless rain. I folded glider after glider. I accumulated several large cardboard boxes full of the things. They whizzed around the cabin. They were all over the place. I hung some by strings from the ceiling. I went out again and got books on origami and some especially large sheets of paper from a printer to make some really big ones. I invented new folds and gliders.

I was running out of space in which to store them all when the weather finally broke. At last the sun appeared! I had forgotten what it looked like.

The cabin was on the rising side of a hill facing the ocean. I began flying gliders off of the deck - one after the other out of those cardboard boxes full. They sailed beautifully out onto the breezes coming off the ocean. One particularly enormous one with a huge wingspan made a complete circle around the cabin! It really happened! Diana was a witness. Of course, it was a small cabin.

Another glider, made of bright yellow paper, sailed way out and down the hill and landed on the hairy back of my dear friend Zeb, our big Toggenburg billy goat. I always thought Zeb was some sort of philosopher, maybe a reincarnated college professor. He was a little startled when that glider touched down on his back, and he jumped. Sorry, Zeb!

But then the paper glider wasn't so much different than the starlings that Zeb was accustomed to giving rides. They would come in for a landing onto his back, too. Often four or five of them perched in a row along his backbone. They weren't just visiting; They were on business! They waited and watched for Zeb's browsing to stir up insects hidden in the grass. Then they would jump down and gobble up a few. It was a funny sight to see them going for a ride on his back and him not caring a whit. I think he liked their company; they kept him from feeling lonely.

While Zeb wasn't all that enamored of the idea, I myself was hooked on paper gliders. He got used to them, too. But might they be good to eat? He'd sniff them over when they landed near him to see. Then he would turn his head disdainfully away as if to say, 'Blah! Worse than that damned spinach!' He hated spinach. It really disgusted him if I gave him any.

> "The cabin was on the rising side of a hill facing the ocean. I began flying gliders off of the deck—one after the other out of those cardboard boxes full. They sailed beautifully out onto the breezes coming off the ocean. One particularly enormous one with a huge wingspan made a complete circle around the cabin! It really happened! Diana was a witness. Of course, it was a small cabin."
>
> —DON GARWOOD

"My friends were naturally curious about these folded fighter planes. They were always asking to be taught, and I usually obliged. After teaching dozens of kids—friends, friends of friends, friends of their friends— I realized that there might be a demand for my brand of folding. It was time to do a book."

—THAY YANG'

THAY YANG

I have always loved paper airplanes. My family came to the United States in 1980 from Thailand. Riding the Boeing 747 "Flying Tiger" to America was my first real flight experience. The cabin of the airplane was enormous. The seats seemed countless— at least to a six year old. I fell asleep after take-off, but I remember landing in San Francisco. A few days later, we got on another plane that landed in Minnesota.

As for paper airplanes, it was an elementary school teacher that introduced me to some simple designs during a summer program. I enjoyed folding the planes, but they lacked sophistication somehow. I wanted planes that looked like the real thing.

Before that summer ended, my two brothers and I had experiemented with a wide variety of planes; changing their shapes and styles. We built more and more sophisticated models. I still believed that a true replica for was waiting to be discovered.

Finally, I tried a move that was to become my standard fuselage technique. I made a giant, inside reverse fold on a model, following with the wing and tail fin creases. I had done it! The breakthrough was simple yet profound. One elementary origami move cleared the way into a world of flying, replica, paper planes.

My friends were naturally curious about these folded fighter planes. They were always asking to be taught, and I usually obliged. After teaching dozens of kids— friends, friends of friends, friends of their friends— I realized that there might be a demand for my brand of folding. It was time to do a book.

It's my hope you will enjoy the beauty of the folding and form of the planes.

JOHN COLLINS

My family lived almost 300 miles north of San Francisco in the 60's and 70's. McKinleyville seemed out of reach of the turbulence of the times, a cultural vacuum—caught in the rug fringe of day to day living. Two dogs, three meals a day, and a war, from very far away, on the t.v.. And something called the cold war... too complex for a kid to comprehend.

On windy days behind the "redwood curtain" my brothers and I would launch a version of the "Flatbed" from the "wind shadow" of our house. If you got the right throw, the plane would go straight up, get caught in the wind whipping over the house and fly over power lines, over the neighbor's field, and over the towering spruce trees a quarter mile away. We wrote our phone number and address on some planes hoping to learn just how far they traveled. No one ever called. To a kid of ten or eleven, that can only mean one thing: the plane is still flying.

The simple act of creating a toy— a flying toy at that— from a cast away piece of material has always appealed to me.

Perhaps having parents who survived the depression somehow imbued me with that ethic. It is certain that my mother, Marie, was the first to teach us how to fold paper airplanes. She introduced us to the waterbomb base, although I'm sure she didn't know it was called that. And both parents encouraged us to explore and experiment with any hobby we might dream up. I liked to fold. I even dreamed up new ways of folding that I was sure were unique in the universe.

In the forth grade, my school had an arts and crafts day. One of the student teachers thought it would be a great idea to teach origami. She must have spent half the night cutting colored paper into squares. (You can find origami paper in Humboldt County now, but not then.) One of the great things about paper folding is the built in accuracy. You can tell immediately if a square isn't square by folding it diagonally. Perhaps it was the timing of me pointing out her errors in cutting. Perhaps it was the frustration of teaching the folding of models she was unfamiliar with. She promptly took a break after I pointed out the umpteenth unsquare, leaving the origami book (by Harbin) sitting there on the table.

I picked it up and thumbed through. There were all the folds I had invented! And so many more. I had intuitively figured some things out, but the array of complex moves— petal folds and sinks— I was hooked. A virtual toy chest could be created with scratch paper and folding.

The paper world is confined only by imagination. A piece of paper is the original multi-media: at once interactive or passive/linear. A pile of blank pages can be foreboding to a writer. A pile of typed pages can make you laugh or cry. A square can be turned into any animal you can think of. And of course, there are paper airplanes.

I'm 33 now— a television director, screenwriter, media consultant, and kid at heart. And I've got a kid of my own. We fly planes in our Marin County back yard. It's a game of imagination. The picnic table is an aircraft carrier, extra points for looping, extra points for a safe landing, and rule changes with the wind— literally. We have stunt contests and time aloft competitions. Every once and a while, we lose a plane over the roof. We can't seem to find it after diligent searching. It seems to have simply flown away.

The question remains: Is the plane still flying? I still have to believe, YES!

"If you got the right throw, the plane would go straight up, get caught in the wind whipping over the house and fly over power lines, over the neighbor's field, and over the towering spruce trees a quarter mile away. We wrote our phone number and address on some planes hoping to learn just how far they traveled. No one ever called. To a kid of ten or eleven, that can only mean one thing: the plane is still flying."

—JOHN COLLINS

Paper

The best paper to use is 20 pound copier paper. The brand found in most office copy machines works great; particularly if it's been copied onto once. Follow Foils need phone book paper, but that's noted in the instructions. If you need more information than this, or if you need to turn A4 into 8 1/2 x 11 ratio, please read on.

All of the gliders in this book can be made from common, every day lettersize or notebook size paper (8.5 x 11 inches or in metric units 216 x 279 millimeters). In Europe lettersize has somewhat different dimensions (200 x 300 millimeters). You'll find that some planes will be impossible to recreate with A-4 and others will have only small differences. It's all in the geometry. By removing 7/8 of an inch (22mm) from the bottom of an A-4 sheet, you can obtain the correct ratio of height to width.

Very thin, flimsy paper, may not provide enough structural integrity. Paper too thick may rip apart when the layers start stacking up on complex planes. There is certainly a lot of room to experiment. We discourage buying paper just for aiplanes. Some people might consider paper airplanes a waste of the resource. Old memos, employee manuals, school assignments or the like work better than unxeroxed paper anyway. The heat process stiffens the paper as does the microscopic plastic coating of printing.

Another property of paper is how well it holds a fold. Some paper just won't take a crease and springs back so the fold opens up. Other papers fold too easily in the sense that paper fibers at the fold weaken and tear due to being folded rather than being simply bent. Then the fold is flimsy even though sharp. Such a fold may not be able to hold the wings out stiffly from the fuselage or keel of the paper glider. As a result the wings will droop or may flap when the glider is flown. So find a paper that holds a fold and isn't weakened by being folded.

The way paper is manufactured usually gives it a grain much as wood has a grain. This is the direction the fibers have been given a favored orientation by the paper making process. The paper is stiffer in this direction than in the perpendicular direction. For photocopy and typing paper the grain is usually in the lengthwise direction.

The vast majority of previously published paper gliders have been folded with lengthwise symmetry, i.e. the keel direction or the glider's center line is in the long dimension. This has been the conventional way to approach paper gliders. In this book, in addition to the conventional lengthwise center line folding, we use a new approach, crosswise folding. In this approach the center line of the glider runs crosswise rather than lengthwise.

The values of crosswise folding are (1) the paper grain runs roughly from wingtip to wingtip, giving stiffness to the wing and strength in its joint to any fuselage and (2) the paper is orientated to most easily make lightly loaded wings having high aspect ratios (wings that are long relative to their mean width or chord). Why a high aspect ratio is desirable for certain classes of gliders is discussed later.

If the gliders are all made from the same size and weight

paper stock then they will all weigh the same. They will probably have different wing areas, so their wing loadings will differ. In fact, since they all weigh the same, their wing loadings will differ precisely inversely as their wing area. A large glider (one with a big wing area) will have a relatively low wing loading. Conversely, a small glider will have a high wing loading. The significance of wing loading and how it is related to flight performance will also be discussed further in later chapters.

Folding Instructions
A matter of valleys and mountains

"No matter how complex a folding move may seem, don't be daunted by it. Every step in folding is nothing but some combination of simple valley-folds and mountain-folds. Most steps are quite elementary in that only a single kind of fold is made. Sometimes more than one fold happens at once. So any folding step is really easy to analyze, understand and execute."

First, there is no substitute for crisp, accurate folding. A well made crease is easier to manipulate than a soft bend in the paper and provides better structural integrity. If you make an error in your folding, and you probably will, make a bold one. Sometimes you can salvage a plane by making a matching "mistake" on the other side of the plane, and then continuing with the instructions.

A valley-fold is made by folding towards yourself. If the newly formed valley-fold is spread open again, the crease as seen from above is a small indentation in the paper. A valley perhaps to something, say, the size of an ant.

A mountain-fold is just the opposite: fold away from yourself.

If this fold were to be opened back up, the crease would appear as a small hump when viewed from above. Or a mountain if you were small enough. One way to execute a mountain-fold is to flip the paper over and make a valley-fold. Then flip the paper back. The mountain-fold is also known as a ridge-fold or a peak-fold.

The folding instructions are broken down into individual folding steps or moves. No matter how complex a folding move may seem, don't be daunted by it. Every step in folding is nothing but some combination of simple valley-folds and mountain-folds. Most steps are quite elementary in that only a single kind of fold is made. Sometimes more than one fold happens at once. But in any case, the step involves only valley and mountain-folds. So any folding step is really easy to analyze, understand and execute.

When a fold position is not critical or accurately located we call it a RAT fold ("right about there" or "relieved accurate tolerance"). But in such cases we give measurements, also, which we have found give good results. This is to satisfy the engineer in some glider folders who might feel that, while it is laudable in pure origami to find folding positions and dimensions without measuring, practical aeronautical engineering can't afford such a luxury.

This book employs well known standard origami techniques: the Randlet/Yoshizawa system. Once you learn this system, you can fold models from books in Japanese, Italian, Spanish and others without reading a word of foreign language. You'll just follow the symbols. They are consistant internationally, and they are simple.

For easy reference, we've printed them on the inside cover of the book.

NOTE: on bases 1 and 2 (on the following pages), the flaps are shown not touching the center line. They should line up exactly on the center line. Throughout the book, layers are shown in this way. You should assume that all layers lline up exactly, unless mentioned specifically. This is a basic diagramming convention used in oragami to help the reader understand all the layers present on a model.

Here they are:

A heavy or bold line indicates either a raw edge of the paper or a folded edge.

A light or thin line shows a crease that was formed in some previous folding step.

A dashed line signifies the position of a valley-fold to be formed in the current step,

A dashed-and-dotted line signifies the position where a mountain-fold is to be made in the current step.

A dotted line shows where some hidden feature lies underneath a layer or several layers of overlying paper.

There are also other symbols used in the diagrams mostly consisting of arrows of various kinds. Their meanings are as follows:

Move in direction of arrow.

Unfold a previously made fold.

Valley-fold then unfold to a valley-crease.

Reverse a fold; squash fold; sink fold.

Turn the paper model over.

A significant point such as when two separated positions are to be brought together by a fold.

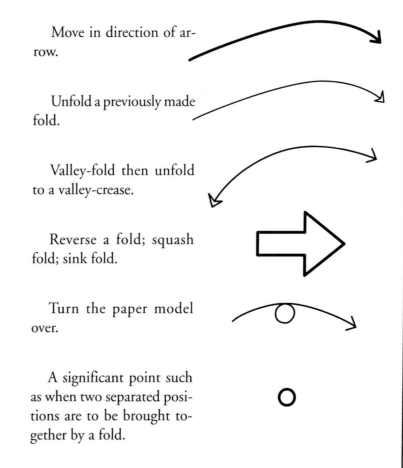

Bases

BASE ONE

BASE ONE

Step 1

Fold in half.

Step 2

Unfold.

Step 3

Bring the corners to the center. The raw edges line up on the center crease Base 1 complete.

BASE TWO

BASE TWO

Step 1

Start with the long side up. Fold in half.

Step 2

Unfold.

Step 3

Bring the corners to the center. The raw edges line up on the center crease. Base 2 complete

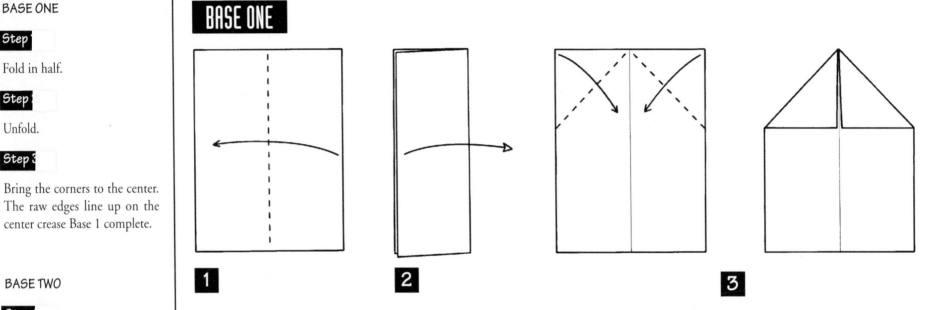

1   2   3

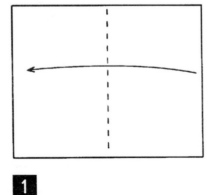

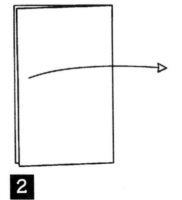

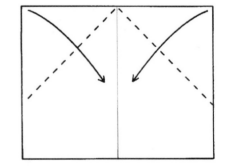

1   2   3

WATERBOMB BASE

Bases 1 and 2 are simple using only three creases. The Waterbomb base involves only three creases as well. In this case we'll need more precise folding and we'll manipulate the creases after they're made.

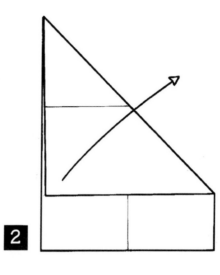

1

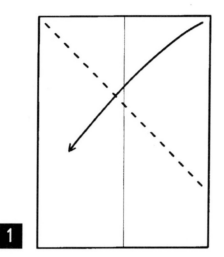

2

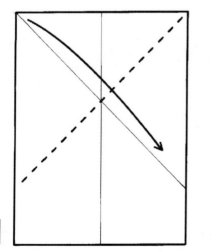

3

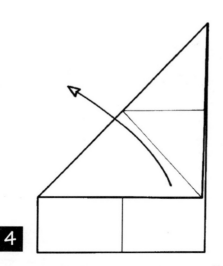

4

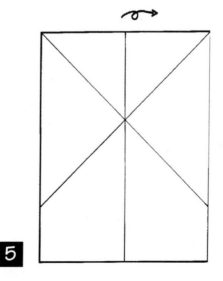

5

Step 1

Make a diagonal fold.*

Step 2

Unfold.

Step 3

Make the other diagonal crease.

Step 4

Unfold.

Step 5

Flip over.

---

* A lot of people have trouble with nailing down diagonal folds. The top of the page is going to end up laying against the side of the page. Start by moving it close to the correct position. Next, really define the corner. Start a crease right on the point. Just start it. Pinch the corner between your index finger and the table or flat surface you're working on. Now pivot the free corner, llining up the raw edges. Flatten the crease starting at the pinched corner. keep the raw edges lined up as you sweep down diagonally, mkaing a crisp fold.

NOTE: There is a center line crease. This is not strictly need to assemble a Waterbomb base, but most airplanes end up having this crease for the fuselage fold.

Make a crease that goes straight across where the diagonals intersect.

Step 7

Unfold.

Step 8

Flip over.

Step 9

Follow the existing creases. No new creases are made in this step. Everything pivots around the intersection of the creases. Start by gently pressing the intersection with a finger. The mountain creases breaks in the middle and both ends come together in the center. The top edge follows the ends down. The whole thing gets pressed flat.

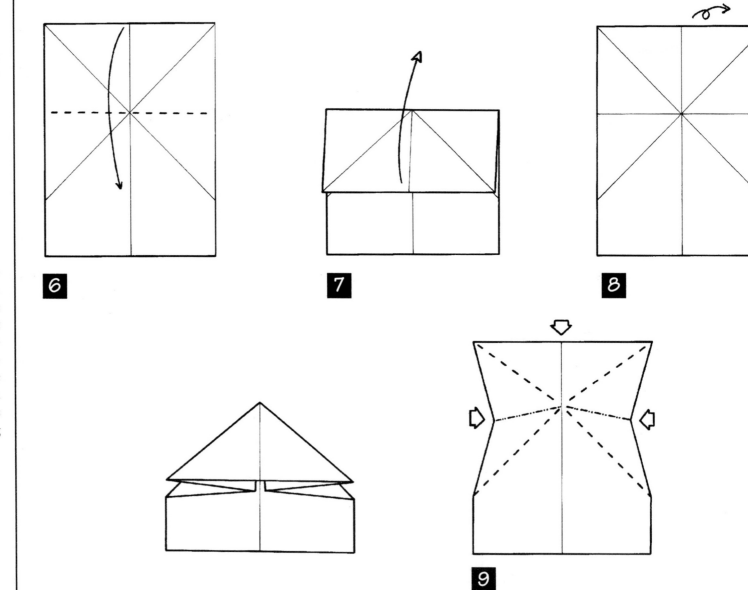

The paper sheet dimensions we will be using are those of ordinary lettersize paper (8.5 x 11 inches), i.e. rectangular and not square (square shapes are typical in classical origami). Often in starting to fold a glider, an initial fold is made down the middle and parallel to side edges. Because the sheet is rectangular, there are two different orientations for this fold that are used at different times, namely lengthwise or crosswise. These lengthwise and crosswise folds are contrasted in the diagrams at left.

A paper glider probably will not fly properly if it is not folded accurately. Folding errors in an early step become magnified as the folding progresses. So take care to make accurate, crisp folds. It is especially important to make sure the right and left sides of a glider are identical.

It's also important to keep the model flat and smooth. Occassionaly, we'll use a SWEEPING move to get rip of layers "bubbling up". Sweeping should be used sparingly. If you need to sweep often, you're probably not being careful or accurate.

Nailing down a diagonal fold: a lot of people have trouble with this. Here's the method I like to teach:

The top of the page is going to end up laying against the side of the page. Start by moving it close to the correct position. Next, really define the corner. Start a crease right on the point. Just start it. Pinch the corner between your index finger and the table or flat surface you're working on. Now pivot the free corner, lining up the raw edges.

In one form or another, the waterbomb[2] folding procedure occurs frequently in paper glider construction. There are actually numerous ways to fold and arrive at a waterbomb construction. The method given below uses the approach of first making preparatory creases and then executing the move which forms the waterbomb—bringing the sides together and flattening the cone. The folding is given for the standard 45° waterbomb (made from an 8.5 x 11 inch sheet, of course), but the same moves are used in forming generalized waterbomb-type folds.

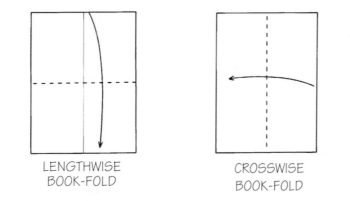

LENGTHWISE
BOOK-FOLD

CROSSWISE
BOOK-FOLD

1. A recent good reference source is S.Biddle and M.Biddle, Essential Origami, St. Martin's Press, New York (1991). Another is Paul Jackson, The Complete Origami Course, Gallery Books, New York (1989). The paper glider enthusiast will be interested in Nick Robinson, Paper Airplanes, Book Sales, Inc., New York (1991) for a concise summary of some folding basics as well as some fine paper glider designs. Also of importance is John M. Collins, The Gliding Flight, Ten Speed Press, Berkeley, CA, (1989). The author demonstrates the reverse, petal, waterbomb and sink folds by using flip-through animation.

2. The waterbomb is also known as the pocket fold although sometimes this latter term refers to an inside reverse fold at a corner.

Launching

"The key to a good straight-ahead launch is to match the conditions at the moment of release to the speed and direction the glider would have flown if it had already been flying! In other words, the motion of the launch should merge smoothly into the motion of the freed glider without any sudden jerks and changes of speed, direction and attitude. Of course, stunt flying is another matter.

Launching a paper glider involves:

1) Holding it in some fashion firmly but gently enough so as not to damage it structurally nor to distort its aerodynamic surfaces.

2) Accelerating it to launch speed.

3) Releasing it to its destiny in the desired direction with the appropriate initial glider attitude presented to the wind.

The key to a good straight-ahead launch is to match the conditions at the moment of release to the speed and direction the glider would have flown if it had already been flying! In other words, the motion of the launch should merge smoothly into the motion of the freed glider without any sudden jerks and changes of speed, direction and attitude. Of course, stunt flying is another matter. But when you want a beautiful glide with no frills, don't violently throw the glider. Instead employ smooth throwing arm and body motions and finish with a clean and well timed release. Launching does take some skill. But this skill will come before you know it if you enjoy paper glider flying. In the drawings of the finished planes, you'll find an illustration that shows how to hold the plane for throwing. This is our suggested grip. Feel free to modify or invent.

Each glider is an individual in the sense that it has a unique wing shape and size, unique control surfaces and particular stability parameters. Consequently, gliders of various sorts need somewhat different launching speeds and attitudes.

Generally, these must be found by trial and error. But some guidelines can be given. A glider with smaller wings has a higher wing loading (weight of glider per unit area of wing surface) than a larger winged glider (assuming both are made of the same kind and size of paper sheet). A high wing loading means a glider will fly fast and so can be launched at a relatively high speed. A glider with large wings has to be treated more gently, for it wants to fly more slowly.

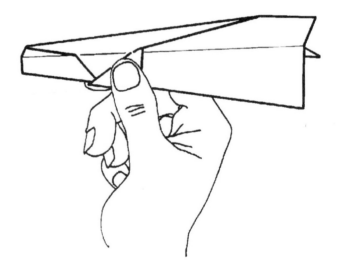

Trimming and Adjusting

It comes as no surprise that a paper shape, our glider, tossed into the air gets pushed on by the air moving by it. One might, however, expect the shape, the glider, to get slowed down by the drag of the air passing around it — to the degree that it ceases quickly to be airborne. But the wings of a glider do something to keep the glider moving. Even if the wings happen to be flat, a glider glides. It doesn't come to a stop and fall (except when poorly designed or improperly balanced or launched).

What you may not have noticed is that the glider's wings meet the air at an angle, the angle-of-attack. It may not have been noticed because it is, after all, a small angle, and the glider is moving away, too. But it's real. The wings then can work to offset the pulling force of gravity. The glider supports itself or lifts itself against gravity. In fact, the drag of the air that resists the forward motion of the glider is overcome by the gravity caused descent itself. Put in another way, some of the energy released in the glider's fall gets converted to forward motion by a wing that meets the on-coming air at a small angle.

Both the lift and drag increase if the angle-of-attack is enlarged — up to a point, that is. Eventually, the angle becomes too large. At some "steep" angle-of-attack, typically around 15 to 20 degrees, the air flow breaks away from the wing and becomes turbulent. Lift is lost and drag takes over. Then the glider does indeed slow down — drastically! We say it stalls.

The lifting ability of a wing depends on several factors in addition to angle-of-attack. The additional factors are air speed, wing surface area and wing shape. We take advantage of this to adjust a glider so it will give a good flight. Thus, with a particular paper glider design (with the wing area already fixed) and for a particular launching speed, it is largely by adjusting wing shape that we are able to optimize lift and select an angle-of-attack that gives the lift we want. So after a glider is folded, it still needs fine adjustment to set the desired angle-of-attack. You won't have to measure any angles, which would be hard to do on a glider in flight. We will use test flights instead.

It is not really possible to develop much understanding of glider flying without delving a little bit into the physics of the thing. As we've seen, proper trimming is crucial to good flying results. What is it that happens when trimming changes the flight behavior of a glider? Sometimes one encounters what might seem like strange behavior from a glider. For example, a glider of the type with a small keel or without a keel might be given some trimming adjustment such that it is expected when next flown to make a turn. But, instead of turning, the glider slews around and side skids without really changing direction much. Why did it do this? Perhaps you are trying to achieve a flight of long duration or of greatest possible distance. What should you do to achieve such an

"It is not really possible to develop much understanding of glider flying without delving a little bit into the physics of the thing. As we've seen, proper trimming is crucial to good flying results. What is it that happens when trimming changes the flight behavior of a glider? Sometimes one encounters what might seem like strange behavior from a glider."

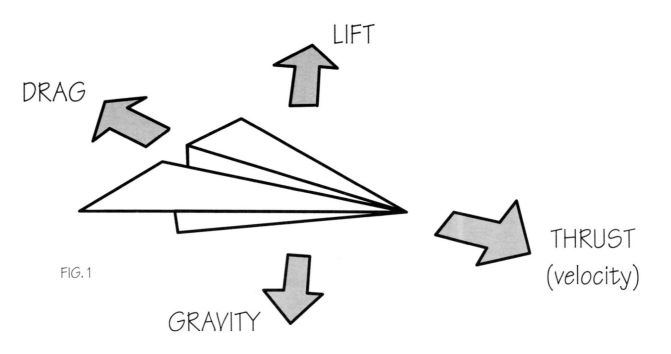

FIG. 1

1. The direction of motion of the glider through the air is 180° opposite the direction of the so-called relative wind. The relative wind is simply the velocity of the air with respect to the glider. The relative wind has nothing to do with any motion of the air with respect to the ground but refers only to the glider as reference point. The angle-of-attack set by a glider's attitude is the angle that the wing makes with the relative wind.

objective? Knowing some of the essentials of flight mechanics can help you at times like these.

A glider in flight experiences two different kinds of forces: (1) the tug of gravity forever trying to pull it out of the sky to the ground and (2) the reaction force due to the mass of air deflected upon passage of the glider through it (the aerodynamic force). It is convenient to split (mentally) the reaction force due to the deflected air mass into two components, namely lift and drag. While differently named, both lift and drag have the same origin in the aerodynamic force acting on the glider. Lift is the component of the total aerodynamic force that acts perpendicular both to the wingspan and to the direction of motion[1] of the glider. The other component, drag, on the other hand, acts along the direction of motion. Drag, as its name implies, is opposed to the velocity vector of the glider and so is a retarding force tending to slow

the glider. These different forces are depicted schematically in Figure 1.

The effect of the two competing forces of gravity and reaction to air deflection may be not only to pull the glider one way or the other. Their combination may cause the glider to rotate in some fashion. This happens when the two forces, gravity and the aerodynamic force, are offset in their respective points of action on the glider. Gravity acts in effect through the center of gravity (the point of static balance; symbolized by cg; also called the center of mass) of the glider, whereas the aerodynamic force acts through the center of lift (Also sometimes called the center of pressure and so symbolized by cp). For stability (to avoid turning upside down), the center of gravity is usually designed to lie below the center of lift. When these two centers are not aligned vertically, the glider experiences a torque[2] causing it to rotate about one or more of its principal axes (pitch, yaw and roll; see Figure 2). The cg is fixed in position by the distribution of paper mass in the glider. However, the cp can move around a bit depending on glider design, angle-of-attack of the wing to air and the speed of the glider. The torqued glider rotates until a condition is reached in which the cp moves to coincide with the direction of gravity through the cg, at which time the torque vanishes. Of course the rotation may overshoot the balance point due to glider inertia, but if the glider is stable it will return to and remain near or at the point of balance or maybe oscillate a little about it.

Let us look at one example in detail. In effect when a glider is trimmed, its aerodynamic design is altered slightly. For example, when a glider is given slight "down-elevator" the wing shape is actually changed a little. The wing deflects more air now due to the slightly dropped flaps. Consequently more lift is produced. Now in the case of a delta wing craft, such as all the paper gliders of this book, the trailing edge of the wing where the flaps are located is at the very rear of the craft (there is no rear tail section with separate stabilizer as in conventional aircraft). The applied trim is a long ways back of the cg, so the cp naturally moves a little rearward. This produces a rotating torque that pitches the nose on the other side of the cg down.

Of course, the rotation changes the angle-of-attack. In this case of a pitch down, the angle-of-attack is lowered. The effect on lift and drag can be profound, as they are strongly affected by angle-of-attack. In general, if all other factors remain constant (such as air speed), lift and drag decrease with a reduction in angle-of-attack. Producing less lift to offset gravity, the glider will begin to fall faster. It picks up speed. Lift increases with speed. If the glider is a stable one,

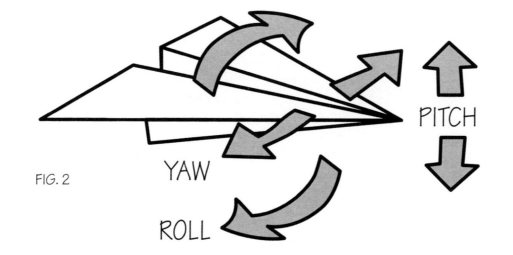

FIG. 2

PITCH

YAW

ROLL

2. A torque is a force or resultant of forces applied at a distance (the lever arm) from an axis of rotation.

3. Stall occurs when a glider's angle-of-attack is too high and its speed is too slow to generate adequate lift to keep the glider flying. For example, a glider will slow down in climbing against gravity, so its speed may drop to the stall speed. Lift is lost, and the glider starts to fall.

L+D	is the aerodynamic force
mg	is the gavitational force
a	is the angle of attack
w	is the relative wind

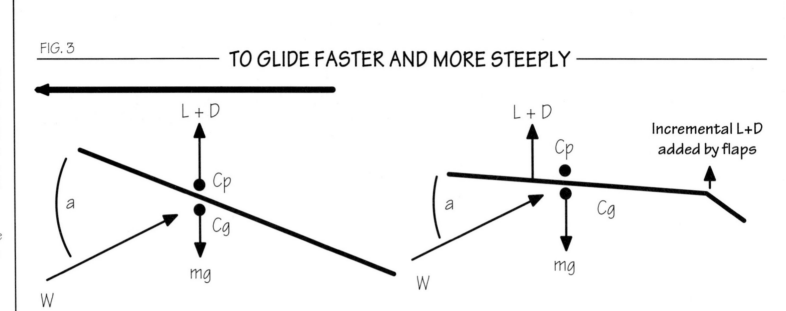

FIG. 3

TO GLIDE FASTER AND MORE STEEPLY

Incremental L+D added by flaps

the changes in attitude and speed will be accompanied by a move of the cp back to being in line with the cg. The glider will now fly a little faster and a little more steeply down.

The above discussion assumed that the glider was balanced to begin with. But one use of "down-elevator" is to compensate for tail heaviness, a condition of imbalance in which the cp is in front of the cg producing a torque that pitches the nose up and increases the angle-of-attack to the point of stall[3]. It should be clear now how the cp can be shifted back by "down-elevator". The point at which the correction to the wing is applied at the trailing edge is quite far behind the leading edge near where the majority of lift is

generated. Intuitively, it is easy to see that the correction added to the lift is at the rear and so moves the cp more aft.

These two slightly different situations are shown schematically in Figures 3 and 4 showing a cross section through the wing at the center. In the case of using flaps to increase speed and to dive a little more steeply, the two centers are always aligned. The new balance achieved after the flaps have been set as shown in Figure 3 is the net result of the slightly reduced main aerodynamic force (the leading edge of main wing has a lower angle-of-attack) together with the increment in aerodynamic force added at the rear by the lowered flaps. In the case of trimming out tail heaviness[4], notice in Figure 4 that to begin with the centers are not vertically aligned; the cp is slightly in front of the cg. But after trimming the situation, now in balance, is very much like that of Figure 3 with the flaps lowered.

Getting the pitch attitude of a glider adjusted so that the angle-of-attack is proper for the kind of flight you want can be crucial if you are in a glider competition. Suppose you are trying for maximum distance flown. If you are flying a dart that does not depend much on lift, you will be using a ballistic launch at a fairly steep angle (around 45° probably) and throwing as hard as possible. Your trimming concerns are simply that the dart fly straight and not turn, dive or climb. But if you are flying a gliding machine you will want, in addition, the smallest possible glide angle (the angle of the flight path from the horizontal). Because drag is directly opposed

to forward progress and because lift is needed to give the time to travel as far as possible, the two forces have to be juggled simultaneously for the best compromise. The angle-of-attack that maximizes the ratio of lift/drag gives the best glide angle. You will probably have to use trial and error with test flights to find this best trim.

You may also compete in a maximum-time-aloft category. Here a soaring glider should have the advantage over a dart. But getting the maximum performance is precarious, which is perhaps what makes this contest exciting. In order to get maximum lift, you will probably be trying to fly near the stall condition and so be risking failure at any moment.

While maximum distance flown is influenced strongly by

4. This is perhaps a different glider than the first balanced one.

L+D	is the aerodynamic force
mg	is the gavitational force
a	is the angle of attack
w	is the relative wind

FIG. 4

TO CORRECT TAIL HEAVINESS

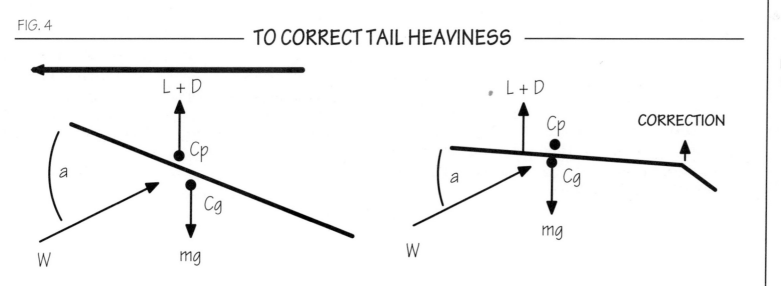

5. By "aileron" is meant a curved or bent trailing edge typically near the wingtip.

drag, maximum time aloft is not. You don't care how far you glide, only how long you stay airborne. So maximum lift (not the same as maximum lift/drag ratio) is required. Typically this is obtained at high angles-of-attack and very slow flying speeds. At this point of its operation curve the glider is on the verge of stalling. Any little draught can ruin the trial if no safety margin is allowed in setting the angle-of-attack. The type of glider needed for this kind of event is slow flying, very stable and with a low wing loading (to minimize its sink rate). But remember, you have to get it to altitude somehow before starting the sinking glide. Such problems and the compromises amongst competing requirements are what make glider flying interesting.

Launching a glider in a banked attitude results in an initially curved path. Some paper gliders can also be trimmed to fly a circular path so as to make a turn even though launched (but not trimmed) as for a straight flight. Simply trim it to roll into a banked turn as soon as it is launched by adjusting the "ailerons"[5] near the tip ends of the wing trailing edge, down for the wing on the side of the turn (the inside wing) and up on the outside wing[6].

The turn usually can be accomplished without any use of rudder. It may come as some surprise that rudder plays little role in banked turning. Air is such an insubstantial medium that rudder alone is not very effective at turning the glider. If rudder were essential, bare bones flying wings (ones without fins) would not be able to turn and consequently would be pretty much useless.

We will pose and then answer some questions about making a banked turn. First, how does aileron control produce a banked attitude? Then, how does banking the glider cause a turn (usually)? Put another way, why doesn't the glider just fly straight ahead in a banked attitude?

It is not hard to see how setting one trailing edge up and the other down—in effect twisting the wing span-wise—produces a torque about the roll axis. The down-aileron causes that wing to produce more lift (effectively the angle-of-attack has increased) and so that wingtip rises. The up-aileron wing produces less lift and drops off. But what happens to prevent the glider from simply going into a roll? In fact, a continuous roll can be initiated by too high a setting of ailerons. But what neutralizes the initial torque once the desired banking angle is achieved so that a bank rather than a complete roll over is obtained?

The glider ceases to roll and flies banked if and when the torque is neutralized. One way this can happen is that when rolled the glider begins to slip to the side. The relative wind changes, now striking the lowered wing more strongly than the raised one. This produces a compensating torque to that produced by the aileron setting and the roll stops.

In the banked attitude there now is a resultant force (but no net torque) which is directed to the side. It is this sideways force that pulls the glider around into a turn , like swinging a weight on a string around one's head. There is also a cost to this turning maneuver. The resultant force is not only sideways but has a downward component. This means that the glider will slip to the side of the down wing. A spiral rather than a level horizontal circle will actually be flown since the glider loses altitude.

Because of side slipping, rudder should not be used to correct for a turning tendency due to a bank. Rudder alone may be able to stop the turning, but the glider will fly in a banked attitude. The slip to the side will cause a faster loss of altitude. Correct any unwanted banking by using the ailerons. Use rudder when necessary to control any unwanted yawing.

Not all paper gliders respond to aileron settings as might be expected. These tend to be gliders with lower aspect ratios. Either they roll too easily or else they turn in a direction opposite to the intended bank! Why does this perplexing behavior occur? Recall that when lift increases so does drag. The wing with the lowered aileron not only experiences an increase in lift but also an increase in drag. In fact, the drag increase may dominate. The wing starts to rise but the added drag pulls towards the back. Meanwhile the other wing with up-aileron is experiencing less drag and speeds up. So the glider yaws in the direction opposite the intended bank. This is called adverse yaw. With the glider pointed in the wrong direction, it can even turn in the wrong way. Rudder can be applied on the low drag side to balance the drag. But even this is not sufficient for some glider designs.

These are some of the physics rudiments of glider flying. With this depth of understanding you will have more control over your glider's flying behaviors. You should now have a better idea of what is happening and how to make corrections when something goes wrong with a flight.

6. If the wing is twisted or one or more wingtips are accidentally already curved unsymmetrically, a glider will not fly straight. Correcting the aileron setting by evening the unsymmetrical trailing edges should stop unwanted turning.

Darts

Left: Patrol Z, Delta Wing, and M-Gun Fighter.

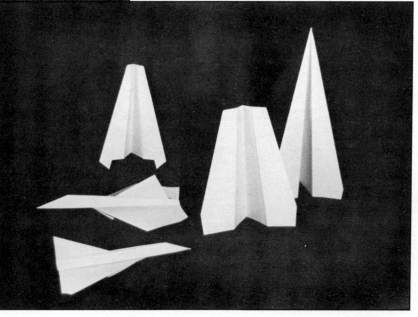

Above: Wasp, Infidel, Dart, Practice Plane, and Mirage.

Fast and accurate, darts are perfect for those surprising speed runs past the unsuspecting bystander. Most of the paper has been folded away for aesthetics or strengthening, leaving small wings and high wing loading. Some darts can be made to do stunts, but their specialty is straight-ahead speed and distance.

Dart

by Unknown

Step 1

Fold in half.

Step 2

Fold the corners down so that the raw edges line up.

Step 3

Fold this corner down to the base. The creased edges should also line up.

Step 4

The creased edges should line up.

The finished Dart.

If you're a beginner, putting in time here will pay off big dividends later. Chances are, you can out fly any fancy design your friends come up with, just by making this one design exceedingly well.

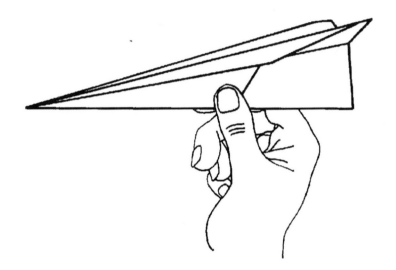

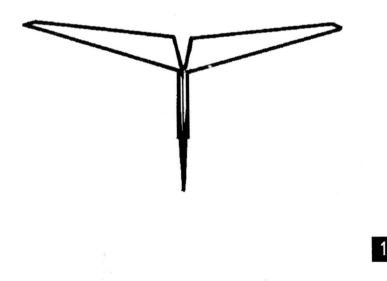

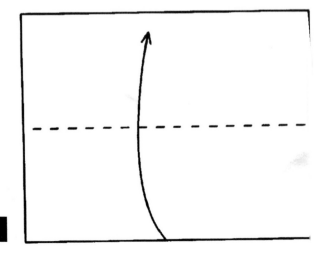

1

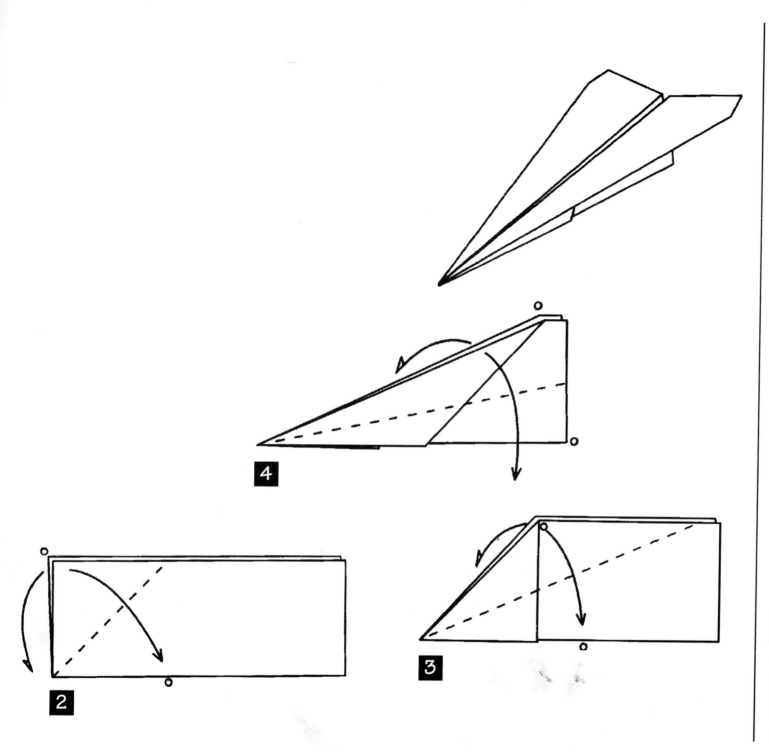

4

3

2

You may have made this design before, but did you really try for accuracy. Did you match up the edges perfectly, make sharp creases, and trim it to fly straight? You should fold a few until they look exactly like the drawings and the photo. Use this design to practice folding technique and accuracy. Precision and sharp creases—these are the keys to great paper airplanes. Use the dart to learn control. Read the "Launching" and "Flight Theory and Trimming" sections and try to apply the stuff you understand. Make an adjustment to the glider and try to predict what it will do. If you are wrong, try to reason out why. Everything you need to know about trimming gliders is possible to learn from this one design.

If you're a beginner, putting in time here will pay off big dividends later. Chances are, you can out fly any fancy design your friends come up with, just by making this one design exceedingly well.

Infidel

by Don Garwood

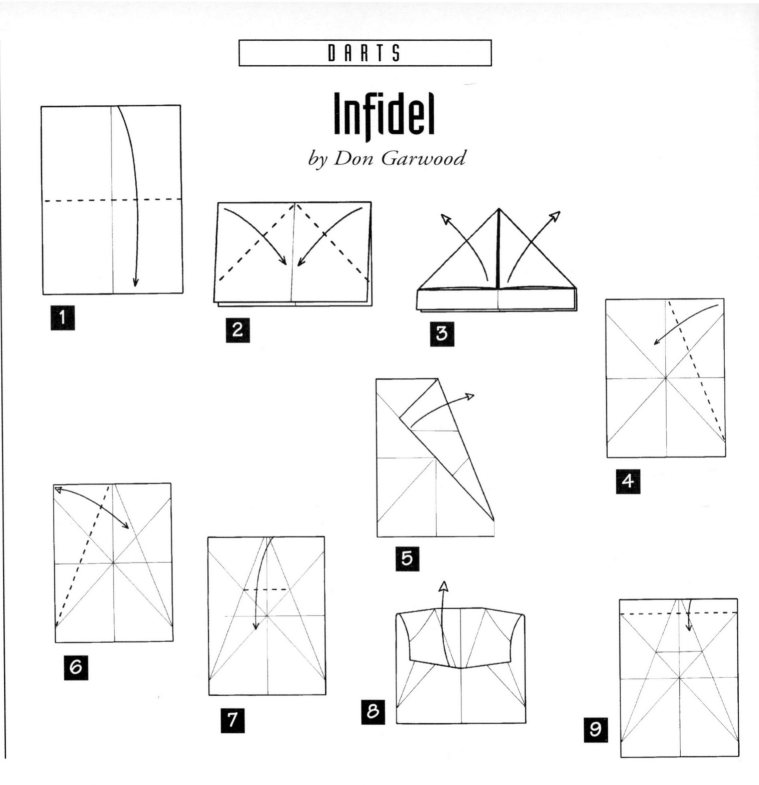

Step 1

Fold the page in half the long way and then the short.

Step 2

Fold the corners to the center.

Step 3

Unfold the entire page.

Step 4

Fold the right corner to the crease. The raw edge will rest against the crease.

Step 5

Unfold.

Step 6

Make a matching fold on the left side and unfold.

Step 7

Make a partial crease that joins the intersections.

Step 8

Unfold.

Step 9

Fold across the ends of the diagonals.

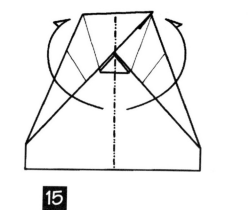

15

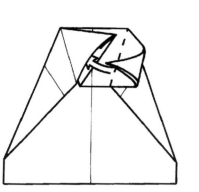

14

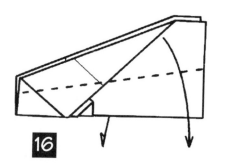

16

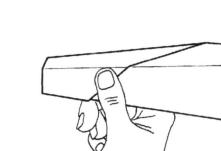

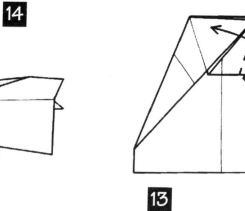

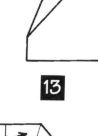

13

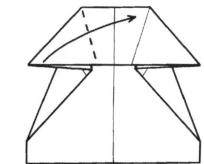

12

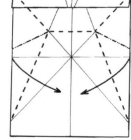

10

11

Follow the existing creases to make a waterbomb-like assembly. The mountain folds will happen as you flatten the model.

Step 11

Shows it happening.

Step 12

Pull up the left flap.

Step 13

Pull up the right flap and tuck it inside the left.

Step 14

Shows it happening.

Step 15

Fold in half.

Step 16

Make the wings by bringing the creased edge to the base.

The finished Infidel. It's one of the many possible explorations of the Stinger Base introduced in "The Gliding Flight". A very fast, very accurate dart.

Wasp

by Don Garwood

Step 1

Make diagonal folds and fold the page in half. Rotate the page 1/2 turn.

Step 2

Fold the raw edge against the diagonal crease.

Step 3

Unfold and repeat for the other side.

Step 4

Make a partial crease, connecting the intersections. Unfold.

Step 5

Make a crease across the points where the diagonals meet the raw edge. Flip the page over.

Step 6

The mountain folds are the only new creases. These form as you press the model into a waterbomb-like base.

Step 7

Shows mountain creases forming.

Step 8

Complete base. Fold this flap up.

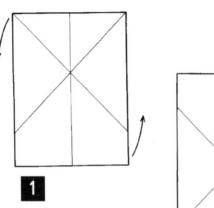

1

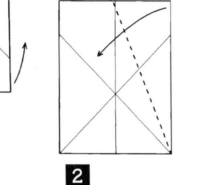

2

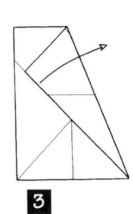

3

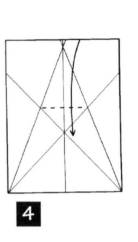

4

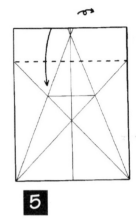

5

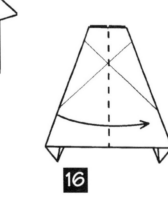

17

16

15

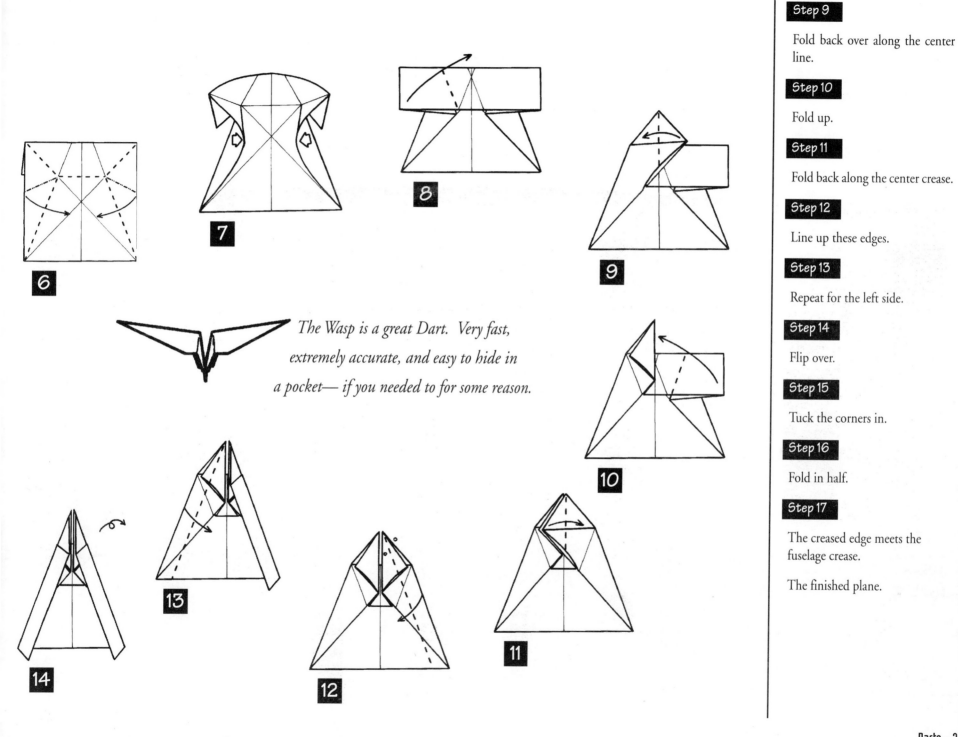

The Wasp is a great Dart. Very fast, extremely accurate, and easy to hide in a pocket— if you needed to for some reason.

Step 9

Fold back over along the center line.

Step 10

Fold up.

Step 11

Fold back along the center crease.

Step 12

Line up these edges.

Step 13

Repeat for the left side.

Step 14

Flip over.

Step 15

Tuck the corners in.

Step 16

Fold in half.

Step 17

The creased edge meets the fuselage crease.

The finished plane.

Step 1

Fold the page in half.

Step 2   Unfold.

Step 3

Fold the corners down to the center line.

Step 4

Fold the creased edges to the center line.

Step 5

RAT fold the creased edge to the inside. Okay, for you ruler weanies, it's about an inch and three quarters down from the tip, and about a quarter inch to the inside of the lower corner. For most of Thay's planes this crease starts an inch and a half down from the tip. So get your ruler out, find a couple of wrinkles on you hand or finger or something that happens to be an inch and a half apart. Study this distance, get used to it. Learn it, know it, live it.

Step 6   Unfold.

Step 7

The same fold happens on the other side.

Step 8   Unfold.

Practice Plane
by Thay Yang

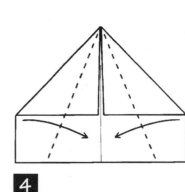

Nobody ever won a war by dying for his country... Sorry wrong speech. The name of the plane says it all. Think of it as a training mission. The Practice Plane contains the fundamental folding techniques found in all the jet planes. If you don't fold this one a few times to figure out how it works, you'll crash and burn later. It's just that simple.

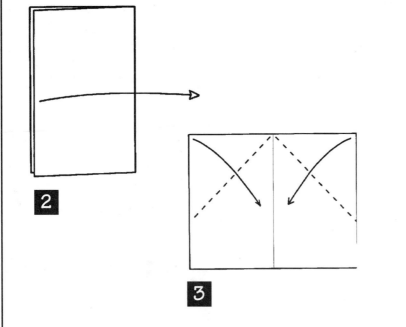

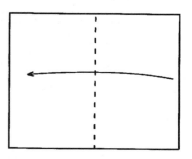

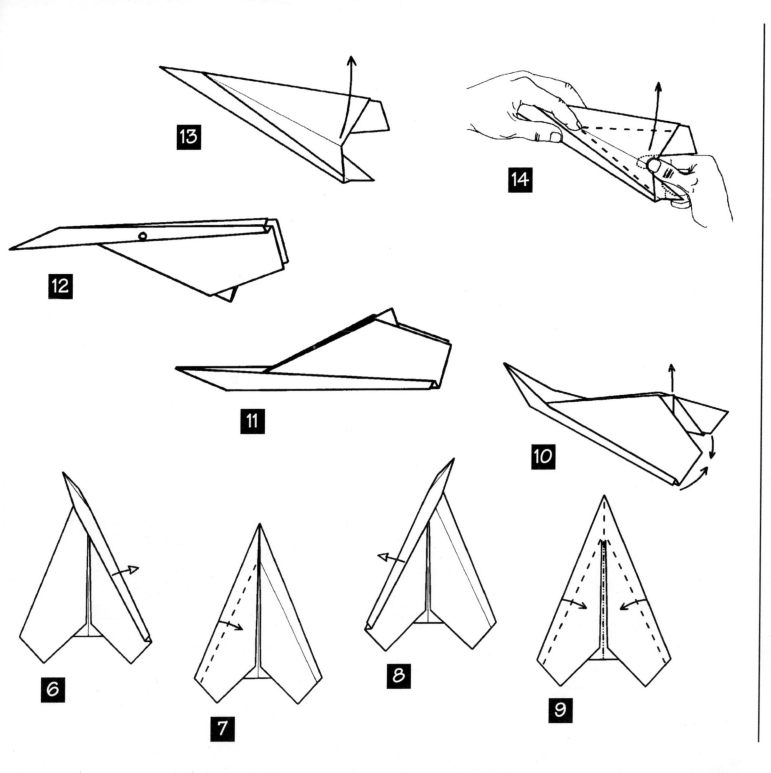

Notice the center line. It's a valley fold at the top and changes into a mountain fold. Pull the mountain toward you and press the sides together.

Step 10   Step 9 in progress.

Step 11

The completed step.

Step 12

This is the fuselage fold that is common to most of Thay's creations. Sometimes the fold in step 5 is parallel to the long creased edge marked here, and often there is a gentle slope as in this model.

Step 13

The next step is to reverse the tail section up. This shows how to start. Allow the model to open like so.

Step 14

Hold the model as shown. The left index finger controls the start point of the reverse (about an inch and a half from the where the valley turns into a mountain), and the right hand pulls up the valley fold and reverses it into a mountain. The dashed lines show where the final creases of the reverse fold should go.

hit the rear corners. Typically you leave an eighth to a quarter inch of breathing room back there. This is important: you're only folding the top layer of paper. Check out the diagram that shows how to hold the plane. You'll see that triangular tab sticking down, perfect for gripping and throwing. Don't reverse fold that up and away.

Step 15

Shows the reverse before being pressed flat to form those valley folds.

Step 16

The completed tail fin reverse fold.

Step 17

Fold the wings up along the creased edge.

Step 18

Now unfold to perpendicular to the fuselage.

Most of Thay's planes will need some up elevator. Bend the trailing edge of the wing upward.

The finished Practice Plane. Fold it a few times to get the hang of it. Also, try trimming for fast, jet-like flights.

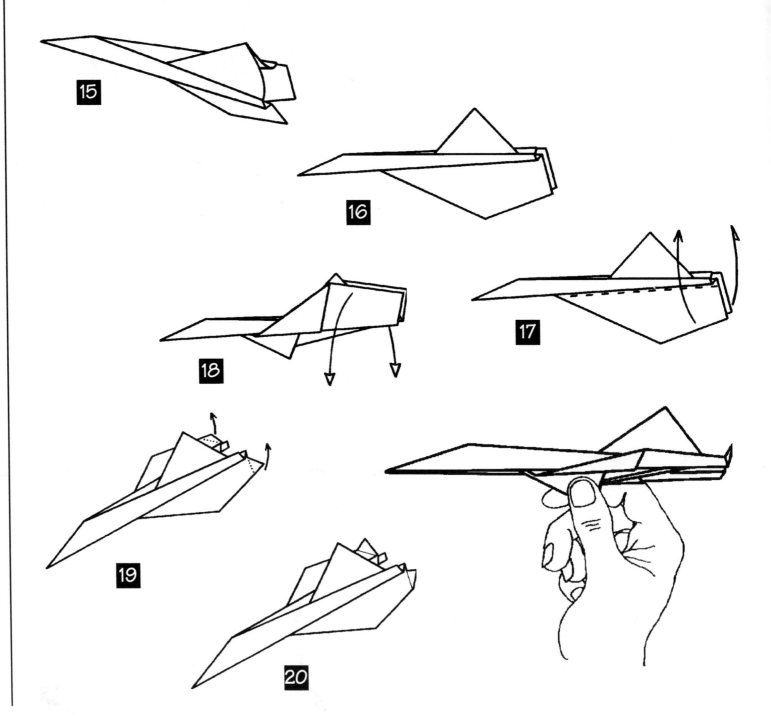

M-Gun Fighter

by Thay Yang

Ste 1

Start with a waterbomb base. Move the right flap all the way to the left.

Ste 2

Bend the corners up and tuck under. Leave about 3/8 inch of raw edge.

Ste 3

Fold the creased edge to the center line. Repeat for the other side.

Ste 4

Fold the creased edge to the center.

Ste 5

Move the flaps to the other right...

Step 6 And do this side.

Ste 7

We're going to fold both points out. The fold starts about 2 and 3/4 inch down from the top—leave about 1/4 inch of the raw edge.

Ste 8

Both flaps done—step 9 is a close up.

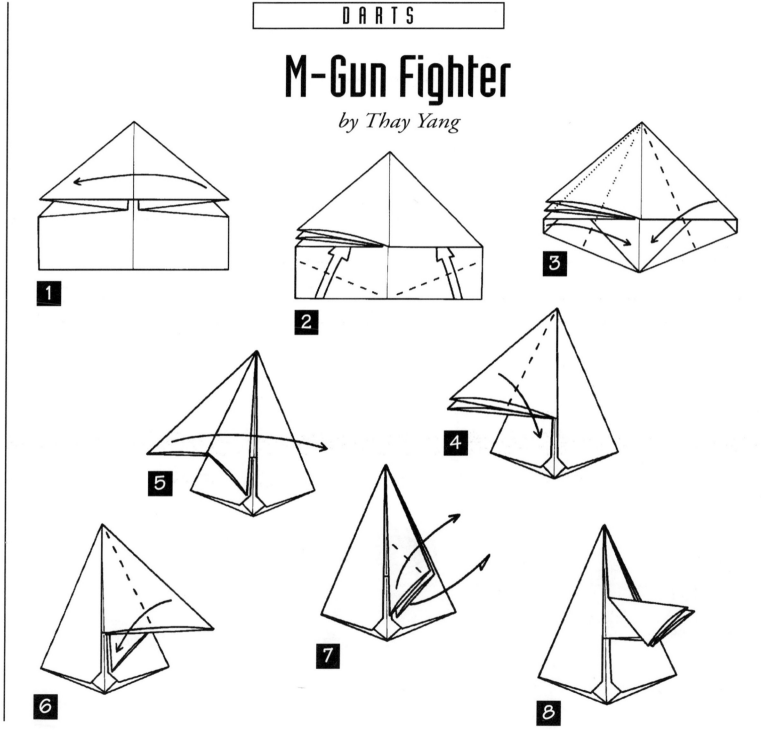

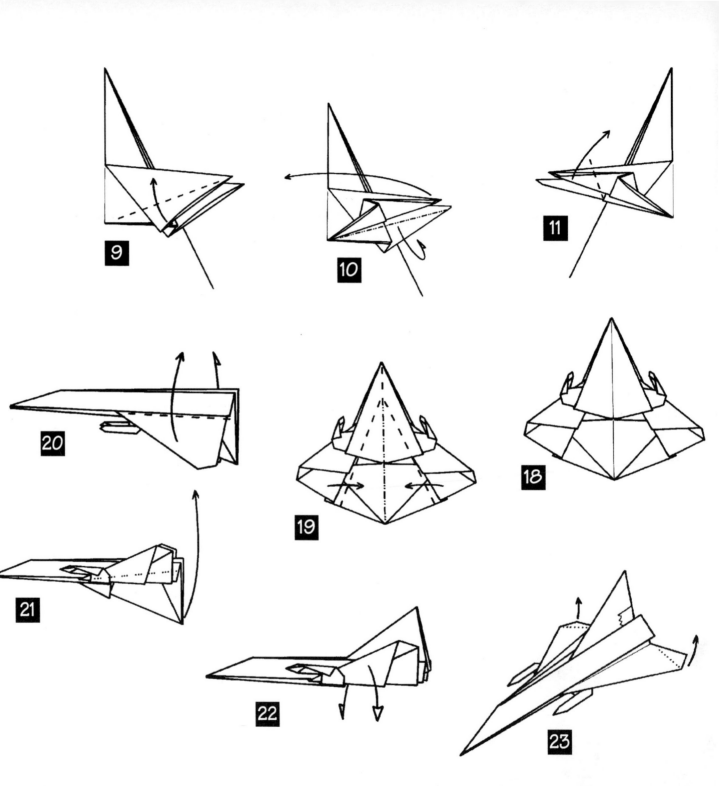

Step 9

Fold up from corner to corner.

Step 10

Do the other side and move both flaps to the left.

Step 11

Fold the top flap up. Note the ending position shown in step 12.

Step 12

Fold the bottom flap away—make it match the first one.

Step 13

Open up the assembly.

Step 14

Narrow the guns with another valley fold.

Step 15

Move the left gun over on top of the right.

Step 16

Fold the wing out—1 and 3/4 inch down from the top; 1/2 inch off the lower corners.

Step 17

Move the top gun back to the left.

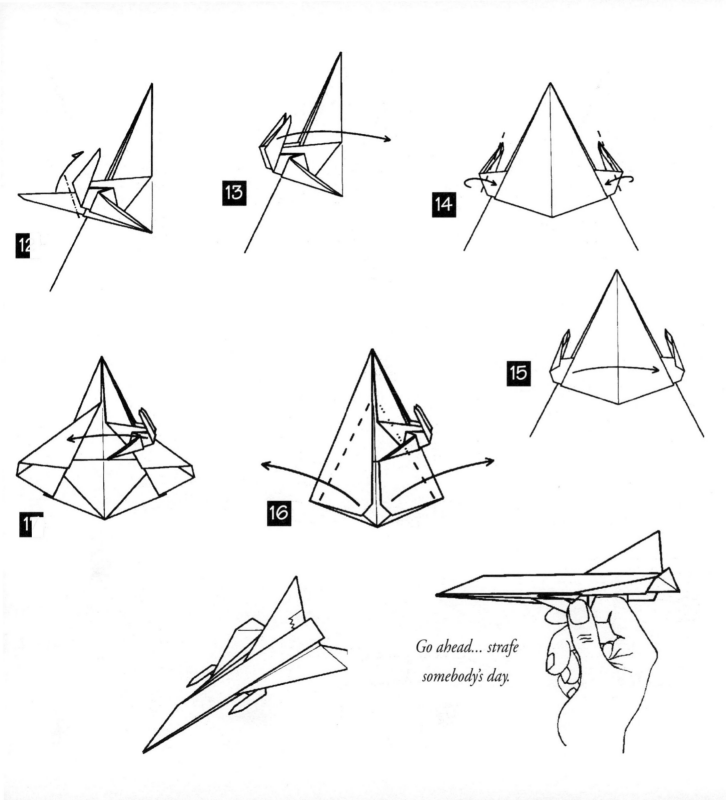

12

13

14

15

16

17

Go ahead... strafe somebody's day.

Step 18

The base— ready for the fuselage folds.

Step 19

Standard stuff here for the fuse fold. About an inch and a half down from the point. Make those valley folds parallel with the long creased edges on the back side. Pull up the mountain and press the model together forming the valley folds.

Step 20

Fold the wing up along the creased edge.

Step 21

Make the tail fin reverse fold.

Step 22

Position the wings.

Step 23

Use a small bit of tape to lock the rear together. Add some elevator.

The finished M-Gun-Fighter. Go ahead... strafe somebody's day.

Delta Wing

by Thay Yang

Step

Start with base #1. Fold down along the raw edges.

Step

Fold these corners together about a half inch up from the crease point. Some folks like to make a pinch mark reference before bringing the corners down. So feel free.

Ste

Fold the small flap over the other layers. (Identical to the Nakamura Lock up to this point).

Step 4

These corners go up, leaving about a quarter inch of the raw edge where marked.

Ste

Now we'll fold these flaps under.

Step 6

They're going.

Ste

They're gone. Put the entire creased edge against the center crease. (both sides)

Step 8

RAT fold action here. About an inch down from the top and about a quarter inch in from the

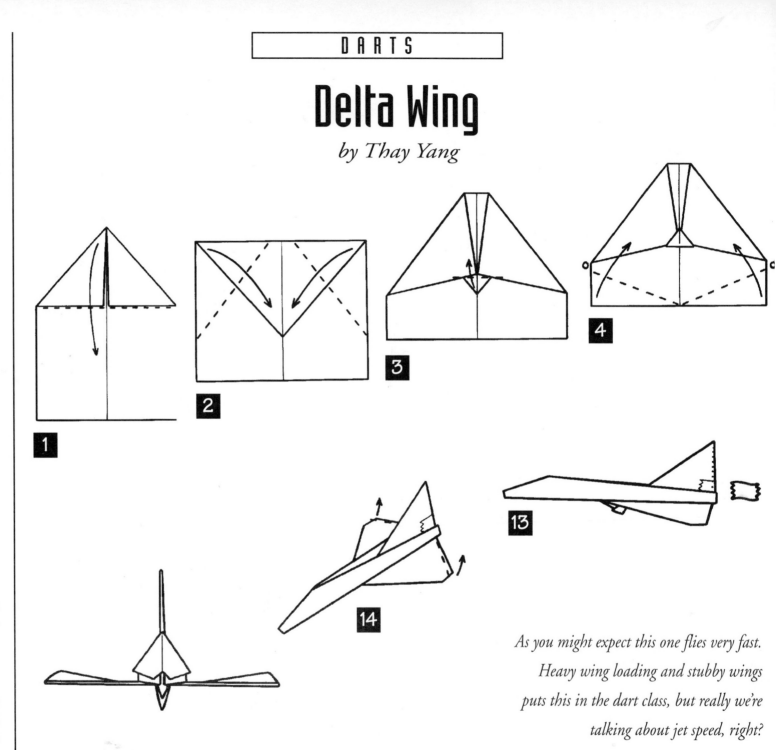

As you might expect this one flies very fast.
Heavy wing loading and stubby wings
puts this in the dart class, but really we're
talking about jet speed, right?

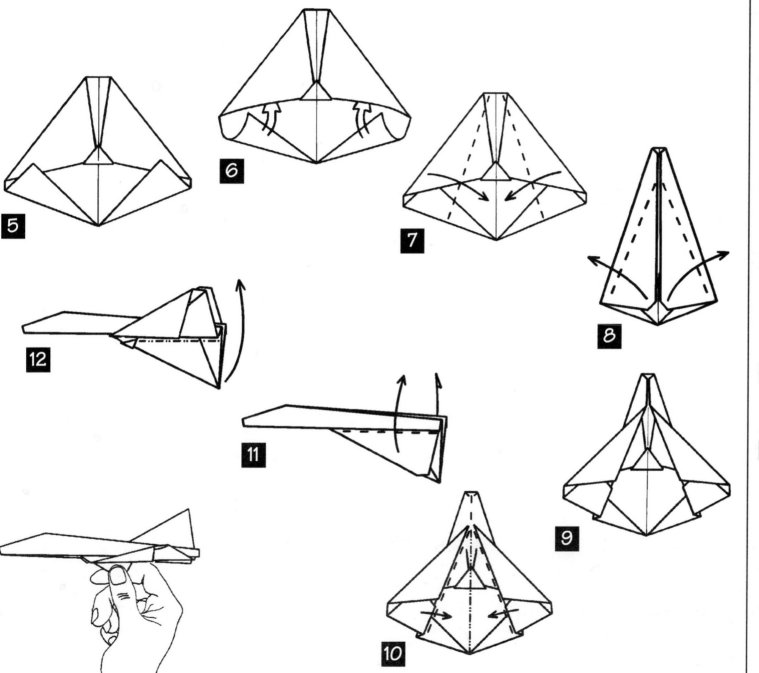

Step 9

Your model should look a lot like this.

Step 10

Pull up the mountain and bring the other layers together, letting the nose valley fold shut.

Step 11

It all presses flat to look like this. Fold the wings up.

Step 12

Reverse fold this point up. Notice the Nakamura Lock assembly remains unreversed. Just let it stick down.

Step 13

Use a small bit of tape to hold the fuselage closed.

Step 14

The finished Delta Wing. You may find up elevator here helpful.

As you might expect this one flies very fast. Heavy wing loading and stubby wings puts this in the dart class, but really we're talking about jet speed, right?

Mirage

by Thay Yang

Step 1

Start with base #2.

Step 2

Fold the corners up under the layers shown. For ruler weanies, leave about 3/8" of the raw edge. Get used to just matching the shapes. Throw away your ruler. Feel the force.

Step 3

Fold the creased edges to the center line.

Step 4

Fold the flaps out. The standard measurements. Try not to measure. Just do it.

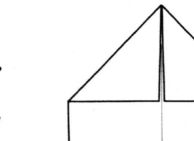

This is a very fast dart, and a fairly accurate replica of the real thing. The ease of folding will make it one of your favorites.

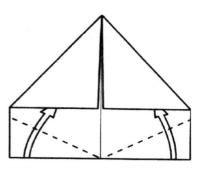

1

2

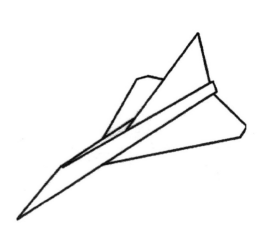

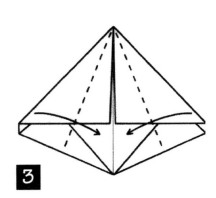

3

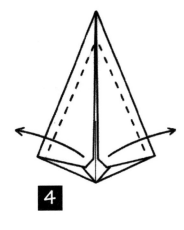

4

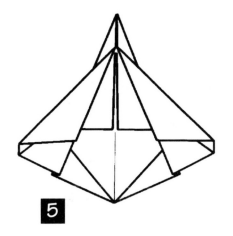

5

Step 5
The Mirage base before the fuselage starts coming together.

Step 6
Standard stuff here for forming Thay's fuselage.

Step 7
Fold the wings up along the creased edges.

Step 8
Make the tail fin reverse fold, leaving the small triangle.

The finished Mirage. The wings have been positioned down for flight. This is a very fast dart, and a fairly accurate replica of the real thing. The ease of folding will make it one of your favorites.

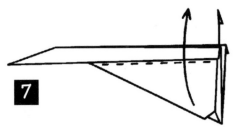

7

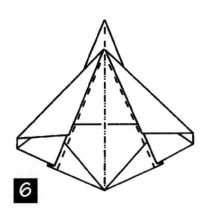

8

6

Patrol Z

by Thay Yang

Step 1

Start with base #2. Fold the creased edges to the center line.

Step 2

Fold the flaps out. The standard measurements. Try not to measure. Just do it.

Step 3

Fold the corners up under the layers shown. For ruler weanies, leave about 3/8" of the raw edge. Get used to just matching the shapes. Throw away your ruler. Feel the force.

Step 4

The Mirage base before the fuselage starts coming together.

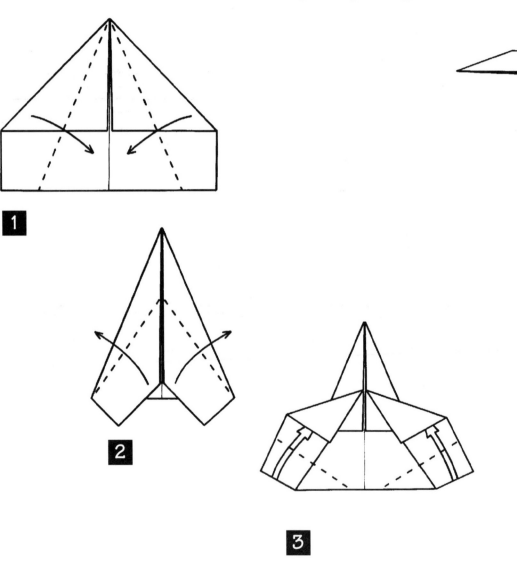

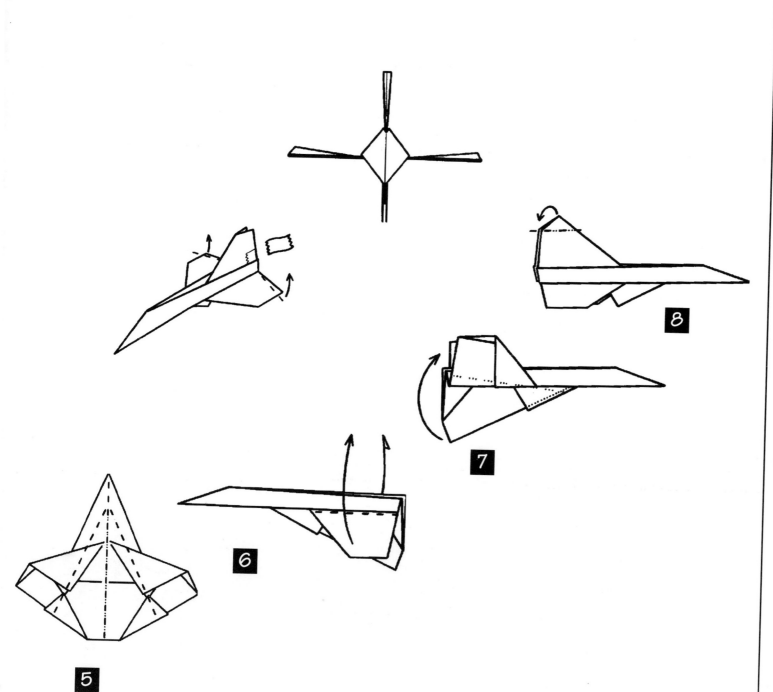

Standard stuff here for forming Thay's fuselage.

Step 6

Fold the wings up along the creased edges.

Step 7

Make the tail fin reverse fold, leaving the small triangle.

Step 8

Reverse Fold.

The finished Patrol Z.

Stunts

Loops, turns, rolls, and flips; these are some of the behaviors possible with the stunt planes. A number of the circle back. Two of them can flip over and fly back upside-down. Some can turn two loops outdoors. One even flaps its wings when trimmed correctly. They are agile flyers, quick to respond to trimming and shifting breezes.

Triangle Junior, Stunt Wing variation, Triangle Junior variation, Stunt Wing, Outlaw, and Intrepid.

Son of Boomerang, Boomerang II, Boomerang, and Wing Thing.

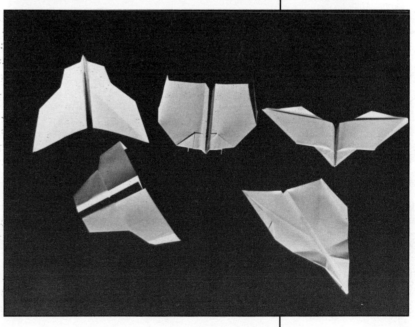

Invader, Looping Lander, Bat Plane, Merge, and Wind Devil II.

Step 1

After making a center crease, fold a diagonal from one corner to the other.

Step 2

Unfold and repeat for the other side.

Step 3

Using existing crease make a waterbomb-like base.

Step 4

Fold this flap over.

Step 5

Fold the point up to the top.

Step 6

Fold this flap to the right—along the raw edge.

We'll do the whole thing on the left side now.

Step 7 Fold over.

Step 8 Fold up.

Step 9 And over.

Step 10

The top point goes straight down to the bottom.

Step 11

The point goes back to the top.

Bat Plane
by John M. Collins

If you flex the center crease and add too much up elevator you will get a flight pattern that almost imitates a bat flapping it's wings. It's a fun plane to experiment with.

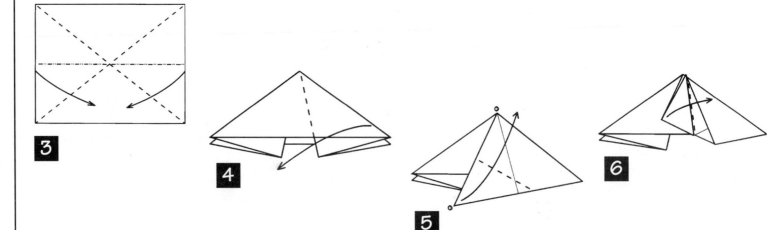

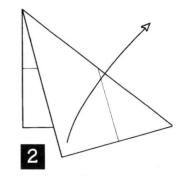

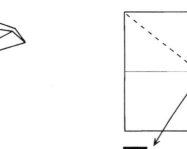

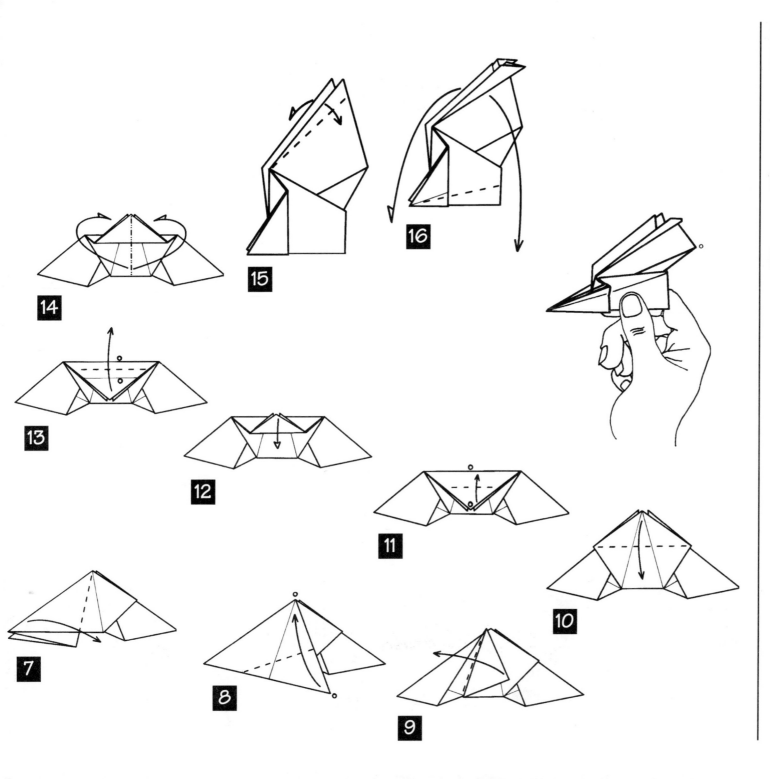

Step 13

Now the crease goes to the top.

Step 14

Fold in half— it's a mountain.

Step 15

Make a leading edge washout fold on both wings.

Step 16

There is a sort of natural break over for the main wing fold. Follow it if you can find it. Otherwise, RAT it in there.

You'll need a lot of up elevator. You can bend up these points until they almost touch the raw edge.

The finished Bat Plane. By Curving the leading edge into a negative dihedral you can get an interesting look also. If you flex the center crease and add too much up elevator you will get a flight pattern that almost imitates a bat flapping it's wings. It's a fun plane to experiment with.

Boomerang I

by John M. Collins

*This is an incredible stunt plane and great glider.
That's a rare combo. It will circle back left or right and do loops.
It will also do giant loops outdoors, sometimes finishing the loop
with tiny flip-loop. It loves high wind or indoor calm.
An amazing aircraft.*

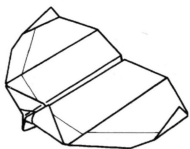

Step 1

After folding in half along the length, fold in half here.

Step 2

Mark the 1/4 point to the crease with a pinch and then fold from the pinch up to the corner.

Step 3

Lift and squash the point:

Step 4   Like this.

Step 5

The completed squash. Fold this flap back.

Step 6

Fold the corner down so that it's just short of touching the point of the pocket. Just a bit of breathing room. And do the same on the other side.

Step 7

Make a valley fold that follows the creased edge underneath. We're getting ready to stuff this point into the pocket, so cheat this crease to the inside as well.

Step 8

Step 7 in progress. Notice the layer curling— just let it do that for now. Once you make this crease, put the point into the pocket and flatten the curling layers.

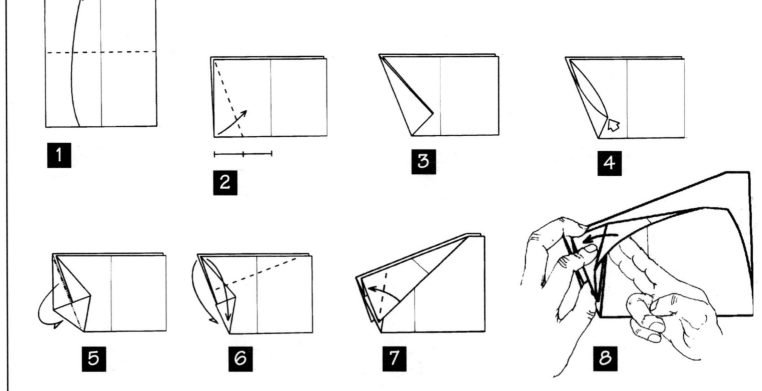

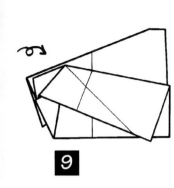

9

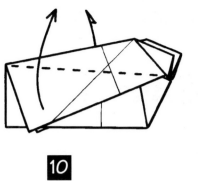

10

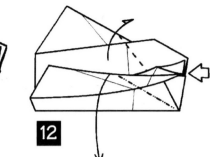

11

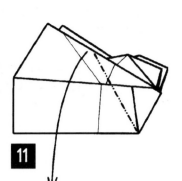

12

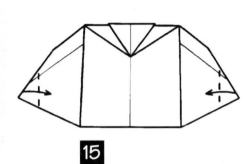

15

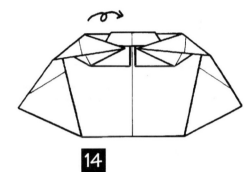

14

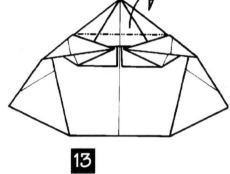

13

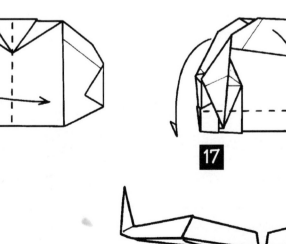

16

17

Step 9

This side done. Now flip it over and do the other side.

Step 10

Fold the flap up— corner to corner. Repeat for other side.

Step 11

The whole model gets squashed. Just open the wings out and press the nose in.

Step 12

Shows the move in progress.

Step 13

The completed move. Fold this point back.

Step 14   Flip over.

Step 15

Make winglet folds parallel with the wing creases.

Step 16   Fold in half.

Step 17

Make wing folds parallel with the center crease.

The finished Boomerang I.

Boomerang II

by *John M. Collins*

Step 1

After folding in half along the length, fold the left edge to the center.

Step 2 Unfold.

Step 3 Fold in half.

Step 4

Fold diagonally from the raw corner so that the creased corner just touches the marked crease.

Step 5 Unfold and squash.

Step 6 Here comes the squash.

Step 7

Completed squash. Now fold the flap back.

Step 8

We're getting ready to stuff the upper left corners into the triangular pockets. In order to do that we have to first get them down there. Fold the point down to just short of the bottom of the pocket.

Step 9

This crease follows the creased edge of the pocket. Go to the inside of the crease so the point will fit in easier.

Step 10

Here's that crease happening. You'll find layer to the right

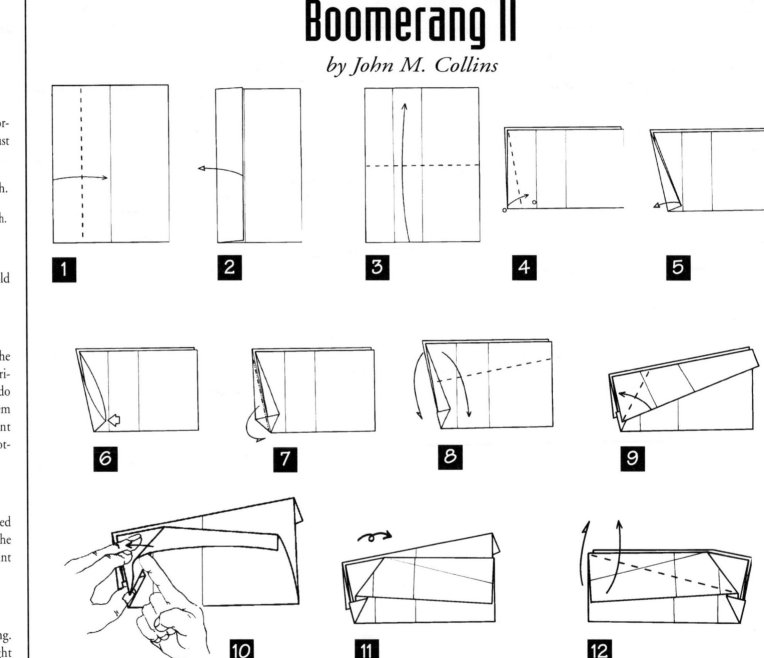

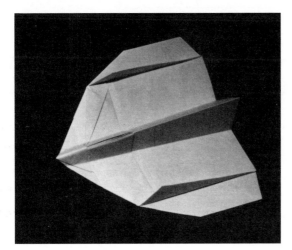

Notice the landing gears get folded down. You'll need to flex the fuselage fold to make this one 'rang. This plane will go out six to ten feet, tip stall, swing upside down and glide back. It will take a little patience trimming, but it's well worth the trouble. What's really happening is that the flexible fuselage allows the wings to open up during the tip stall. This creates enough negative dihedral that the plane can fly upside down. It's a delicate balance having enough up elevator or positive dihedral to stall, and still be able to fly upside down on return. Precise folding is a must. There's not a lot of room for error, and the trick only works indoors. When you master this one, your friends will be truly amazed, and they'll never figure it out.

bending. Let it bend while you stuff the point into the pocket. Then flatten the bending layer.

Step 11

Flip over and do the whole enchilada again.

Step 12

Fold up corner to corner.

Step 13

Open up this puppy and squash it flat.

Step 14

The squash in progress.

Step 15

Fold the creased edgers over, lining them up with the layer underneath. A completed squash.

Step 16

Make the winglets roughly parallel with the crease edge. Some folks like to wait and do winglets last. You can too if you like.

Step 17
Fold in half.

Step 18

Make wing folds. A very gentle slope. Notice where the crease starts at the nose—just off that small triangle.

The finished Boomerang II.

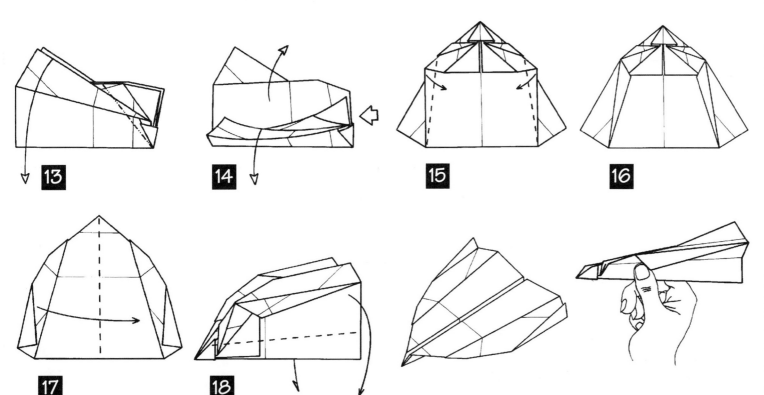

Son of Boomerang

by John M. Collins

Step 1

Fold the page in half.

Step 2

Fold the corners down.

Step 3

Open up the center crease.

Step 4

The tip hits the hidden corners.

Step 5   Refold in half.

Step 6

The front creased edge meets the bottom.

Step 7

Creased edge meets the bottom.

Step 8

Unfold the top side only.

Step 9

Fold the top side down so that the new crease meets this corner.

Step 10

Now make the other side match.

Step 11

Open up the wings.

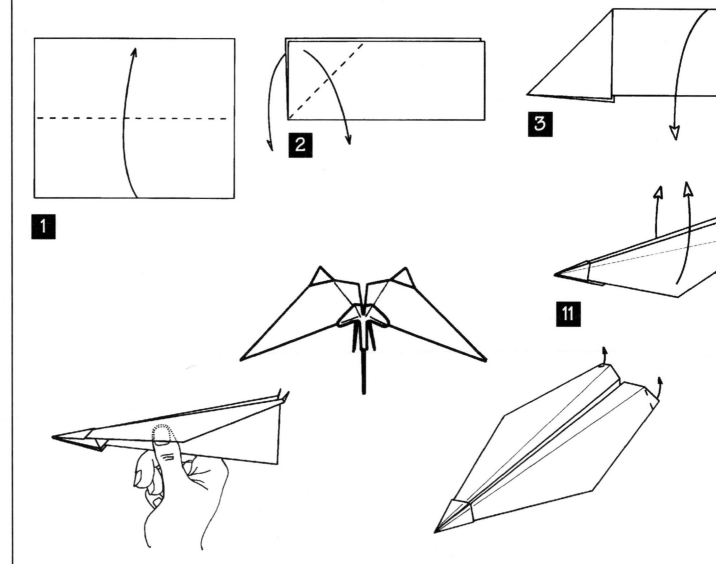

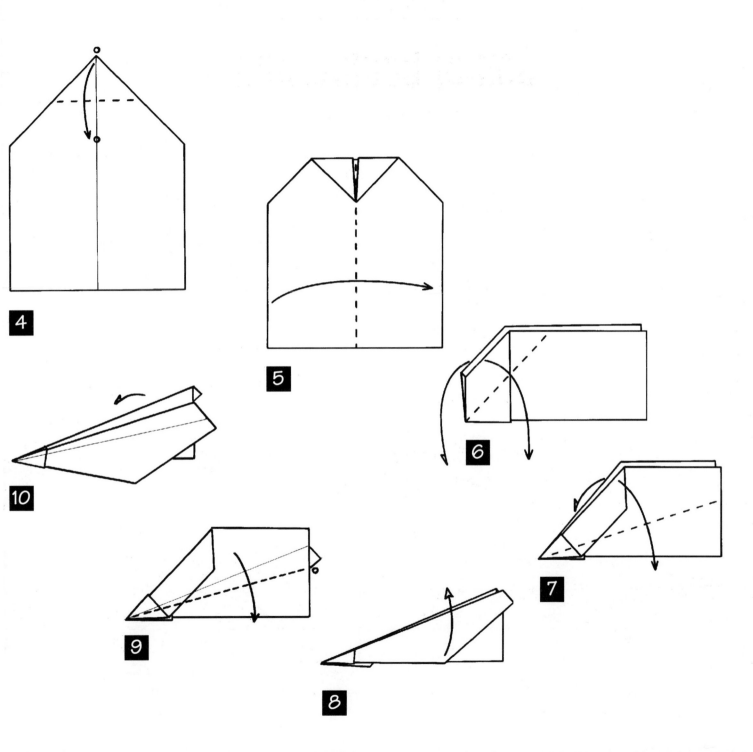

4

5

6

7

8

9

10

The finished Son of Boomerang. Set the wing creases like the diagrams. You'll also need some up elevator to get the correct stall. Also, flex the center crease to make the wings open up easily. The trick is to get it to tip stall so that the nose goes up stops at near vertical and swings back down, continueing around until it points back at you with the airplane upside down. The wings should be flexed open at this point, allowing the plane to glide back to you upside down. It will only travel out about five feet or so before stalling.

Although Son of Boomerang is easier to build than Boomerang II, it is not as reliable in flight path. With patient adjustment you can accomplish the feat.

Looping Lander

by John M. Collins

Step 1

The waterbomb base is the beginning. Fold the tip down to the base of the triangle.

Step 2 Fold up the points

Step 3

Unfold to the waterbomb base.

Step 4

Fold the points to the center.

Step 5 Unfold.

Step 6

This is like a petal fold, sort of. Using existing creases, pull the raw edge up and let the sides come in.

Step 7

The completed step. Reverse fold these corners.

Step 8

Fold three points down.

Step 9

Fold the tip down to the intersection.

Step 10 Unfold.

Step 11

The dreaded sink fold. You have to open up the model:

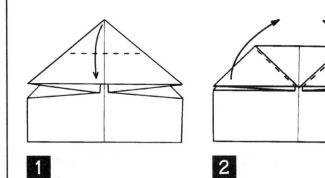

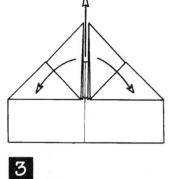

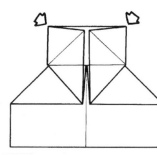

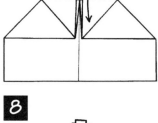

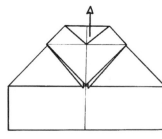

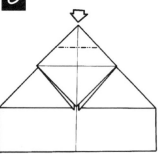

1

2

3

4

5

6

7

8

9

10

11

You can get tighter loops by making the winglets larger or by adding extra up elevator. With the right toss, you should get a nice round loop and a smooth landing.

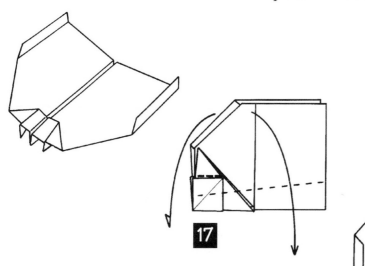

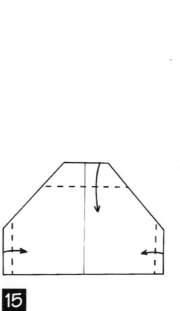

17

16

15

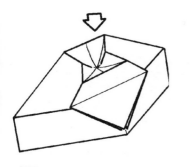

12

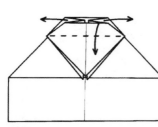

13

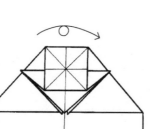

14

Step 12

Like this— the point is already pressed down here. Now press it flat again.

Step 13

Piece of cake right? Pull the front forward and allow the inner layers to flatten out.

Step 14   Flip over.

Step 15

Fold this flap back along the natural break over. You can also make the winglets now. They can be made up to twice the size show for tighter looping.

Step 16   Fold in half.

Step 17

Make the wing fold by starting half way up the side of the square shape and sloping up toward the rear. Also bend the landing gear down.

The finished Looping Lander. You can get tighter loops by making the winglets larger or by adding extra up elevator. With the right toss, you should get a nice round loop and a smooth landing.

Wing Thing

by John M. Collins

Step 1

Book fold and then bring the right corner to the bottom.

Step 2

Unfold and repeat for the other side.

Step 3

Make a mountain fold across the intersection and then follow the existing creases to make a waterbomb-like base.

Step 4 The completed base.

Step 5

Pull the top corner out to the creased edge and make a new set of creases.

Step 6

One side done. Now do the other.

Step 7

Basically were just squashing this corner. Use the raw edge marked with the valley fold as a guide for the squash.

Step 8 Step 7 in progress.

Step 9

Completed squash. Now cook the other side.

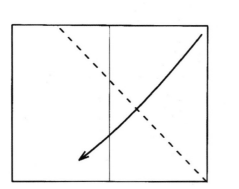

1

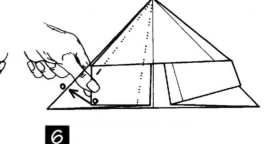

2

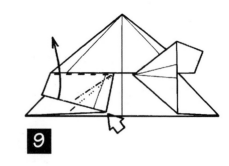

3

4

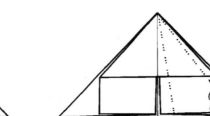

5

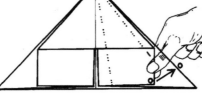

6

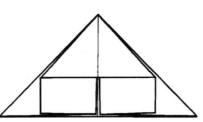

7

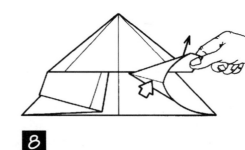

8

9

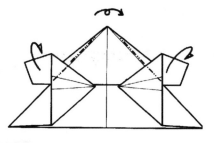

10

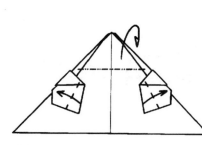

11

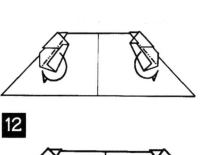

12

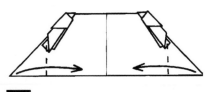

13

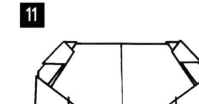

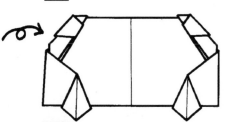

14

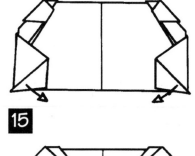

15

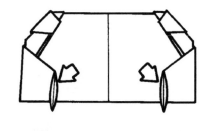

16

17

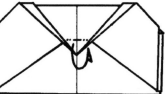

18

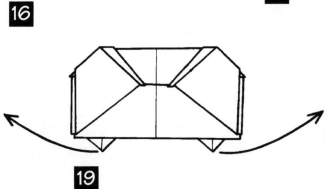

19

Step 10

Fold along the big creased edge. The flip over.

Step 11

Fold the raw edges up so they look like the next drawing. Also fold the top point back.

Step 12

Now fold these flaps under.

Step 13

Fold the outside points toward the center. Depending on the thickness of your paper, you may want to stop where the drawing shows or fold all the way to the center.

Step 14

Fold the points back out to the corners.

Step 15

Pull these points up and:

Step 16 — Squash them down.

Step 17 — Flip it over.

Step 18

Tuck this point under.

Step 19

Stretch the thing out.

The finished Wing Thing.

Merge

by Don Garwood

Step 1

Fold in half along the length and width. With a long side on top, make a crease that starts at the lower left corner by moving the upper left corner to the marked crease.

Step 2

Fold back along the center line.

Step 3

We'll repeat 1 and 2 for the right side. Notice how you can match up the corners for step 1.

Step 4

Then fold back along the center line.

Step 5

Fold the top back across where the flaps end.

Step 6

To make this fold look at step 7 and notice how far the corners extend past the raw edge. Notice how the raw edge touches the center of the creased edge. That's how you line up these creases.

Step 7   Tuck these points under.

Step 8   Flip over.

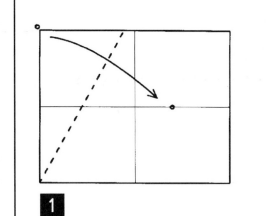

1

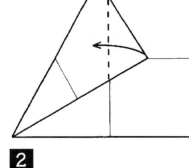

2

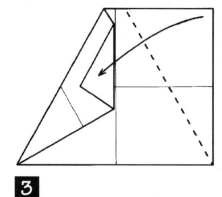

3

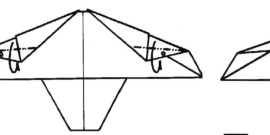

6

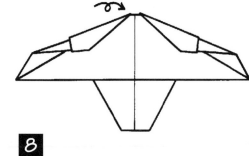

7

8

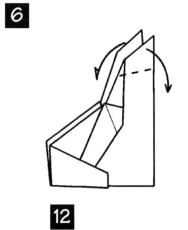

12

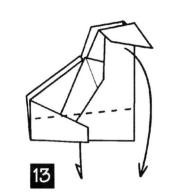

13

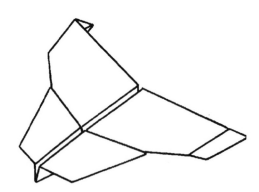

A fine Leading Edge Extension Delta Wing glider.
The wing loading on this plane makes it ideal
indoors or out. Trim for looping or circling.

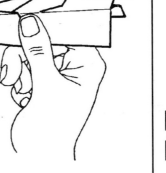

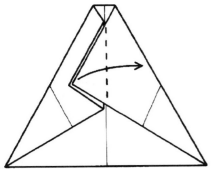

4

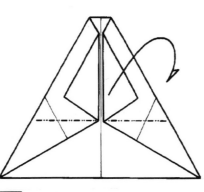

5

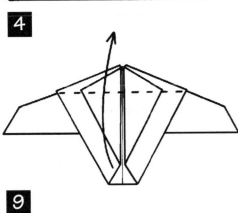

9

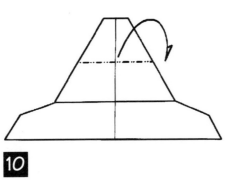

10

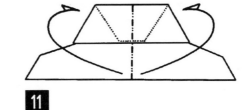

11

Step 9 Fold the flap up.

Step 10

Mountain fold the flap in half.

Step 11

Fold the plane in half.

Step 12

Fold and unfold the winglets.

Step 13

Make the wing folds by starting about half way up the front edge and ending just short of the height of the front edge at the rear.

The finished Merge. A fine Leading Edge Extension Delta Wing glider. The wing loading on this plane makes it ideal indoors or out. Trim for looping or circling.

Step

After folding in half along the length, bring the top of the page to the bottom.

Step 2

Fold the corners to the center.

Step 3   Unfold.

Step 4

Fold the top down. Crease across the ends of the diagonals.

Step 5

Waterbomb with existing creases.

Step 6

Fold this flap up so that the creased edge is horizontal and the point just touches the other creased edge.

Ste

The same fold here.

Step 8   Unfold.

Step 9

Fold the top down across the ends of the creases.

Step 10

Fold the raw edges to the creases.

Stunt Wing

by Don Garwood

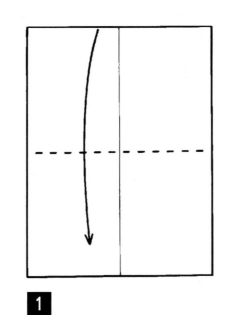

1

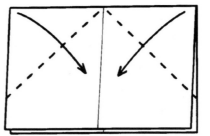

2

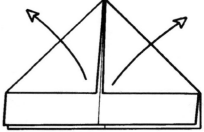

3

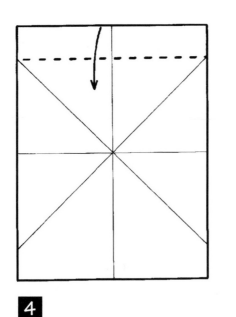

4

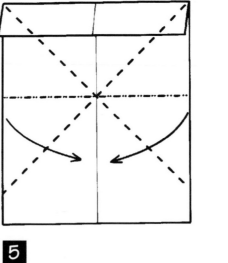

5

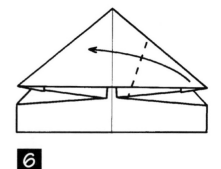

6

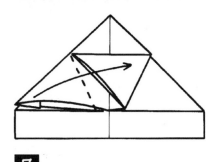
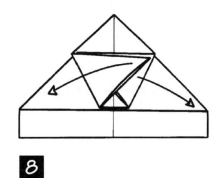
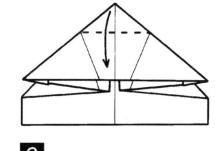

7

8

9

Step 11

Now remake the creases, tucking the points into the pockets.

Step 12

Fold the creases edges to the pocket assembly.

Step 13 Unfold.

Step 14

This is an alternative wing fold.

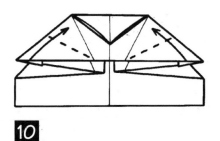
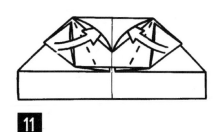
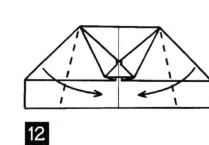

10

11

12

The finished Stunt Wing. This will loop or circle back depending on trim and adjustment of the wing droop. You'll need to play with setting the wing creases at the correct angles. The diagrams and photos are very accurate. Notice the different launching technique as well. A very well built, fun stunt plane.

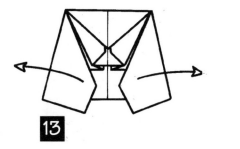
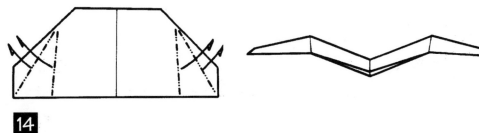

13

14

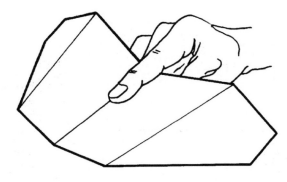

This will loop or circle back depending on trim and adjustment of the wing droop. You'll need to play with setting the wing creases at the correct angles. A very well built, fun stunt plane.

Triangle Junior

by Don Garwood

Step 1

Start with a waterbomb base. Fold the crease edges to the center.

Step 2

Fold the point down.

Step 3

Fold the top creased edges to the center.

Step 4

The glider so far. We're going to tuck those protruding flaps into the model.

Ste

Here we go. Lift one side, valley fold the flap up and into the pocket area, and then let the whole thing flatten. Repeat for the other side.

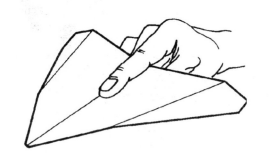

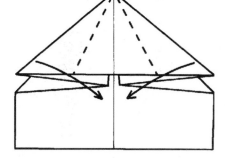

1

2

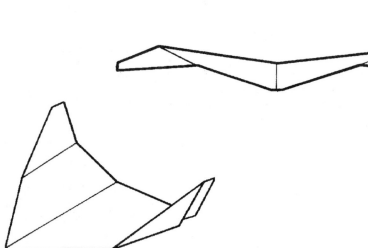

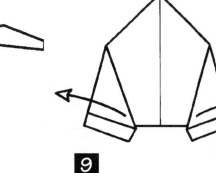

9

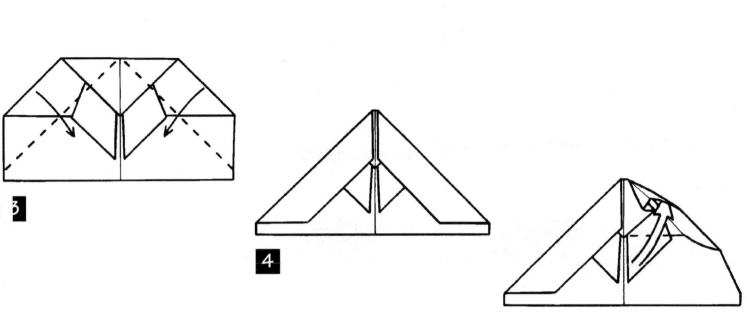

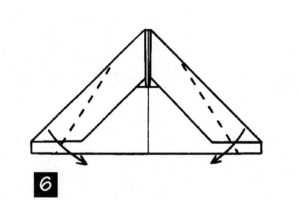

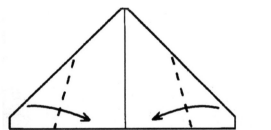

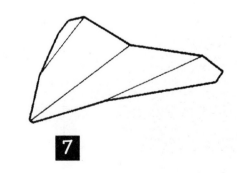

Step 6

There is a natural "break-over" point where the crease starts by the nose. The crease finishes through a point just off the mid-point of the small raw edge.

Step 7

Unfold for one possible wing configuration.

Step 8

You could flip the model over and use the same break over point. This time make larger flaps.

Step 9

The flaps can eat up a little more than a third of their respective wings.

The finished Triangle Junior shown with both wing options.

Either one will be a joy to fly.

Intrepid

by Don Garwood

Step

Start with base #1. Unfold the flaps.

Step 2

Fold a long diagonal fold so that the raw edge marked touches the crease marked.

Step 3

Unfold and repeat for the other side.

Step 4

Fold up across the intersection.

Step 5 Unfold.

Step 6

Fold the corner down so that the corner and the raw edge line up with the crease from step 4.

Step 7

Unfold and repeat for the other side.

Step 8

Now a fold similar to step 2. The raw edge will rest on the crease.

Step 9

Unfold and repeat for the other side.

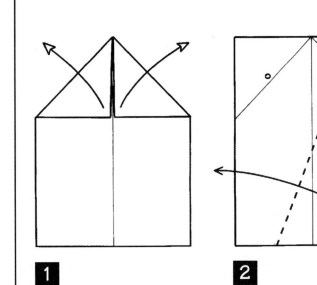

1

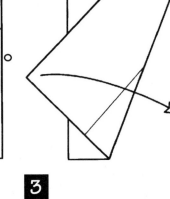

2

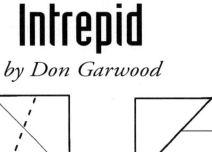

3

4

5

6

7

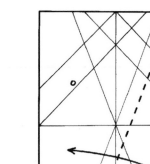

8

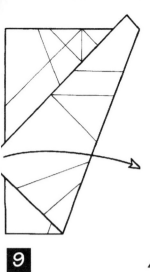

9

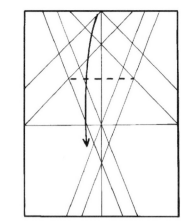

10

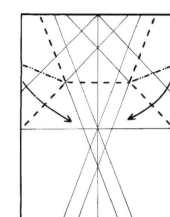

11

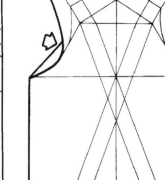

12

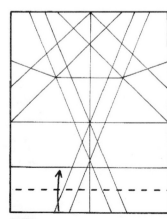

13

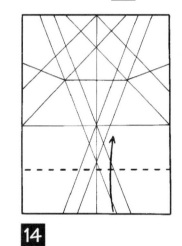

14

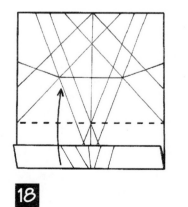

15

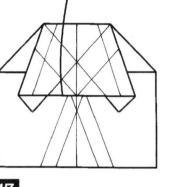

16

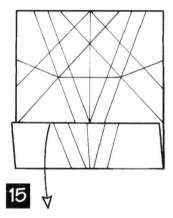

17

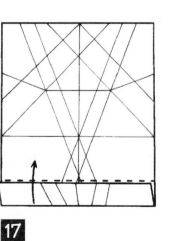

18

Step 10

Make a crease that connects the intersections and unfold.

Step 11

Follow existing creases with valley folds. By pressing them into a waterbomb-like base, the mountain folds form.

Step 12

Shows the move in progress.

Step 13

The completed assembly. Egads! Unfold again!

Step 14

Fold the raw edge up to meet the crease.

Step 15   Unfold.

Step 16

Fold the raw edge to the new crease.

Step 17

Fold up again. Follow an existing crease.

Step 18

Follow another existing crease.

Step 19

It's not the completed plane, but you deserved a break.

Step 20

We follow the creases on the bottom layer to assemble a waterbomb-like base.

Step 21 Flip me over.

Step 22

Pull the right flap over to the left.

Step 23

Pull the left flap over and put it inside the other.

Step 24

Flip me over again.

Step 25

Mountain fold where shown.

The finished Intrepid. Notice the curving of the wing. It's almost a flat dihedral, with the curve counting for most of it. Also notice that the mountain folds from step 25 are very subtle. You can adjust these for right or left turning. Trim for flat glides or spectacular loops. You should also get the Intrepid to circle back to you by launching it banked right or left.

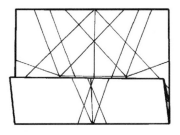
19

20

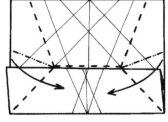
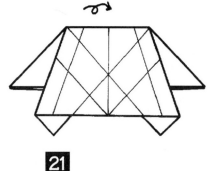
21

22

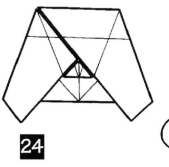
23

24

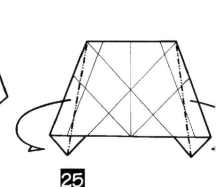
25

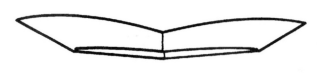

Invader

by Don Garwood

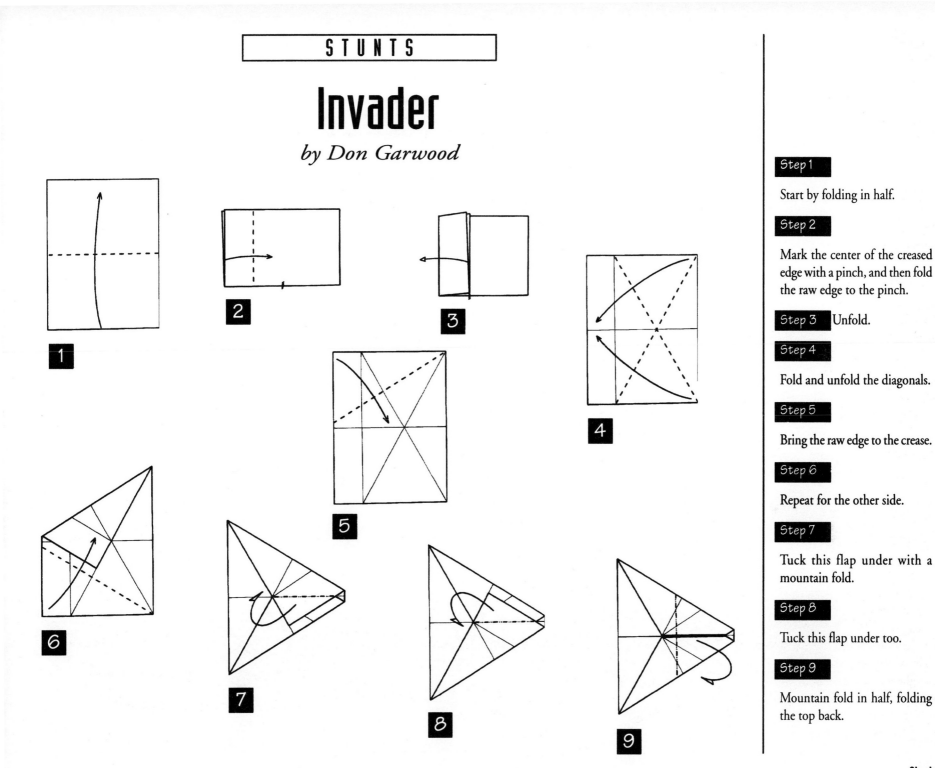

Step 1

Start by folding in half.

Step 2

Mark the center of the creased edge with a pinch, and then fold the raw edge to the pinch.

Step 3 Unfold.

Step 4

Fold and unfold the diagonals.

Step 5

Bring the raw edge to the crease.

Step 6

Repeat for the other side.

Step 7

Tuck this flap under with a mountain fold.

Step 8

Tuck this flap under too.

Step 9

Mountain fold in half, folding the top back.

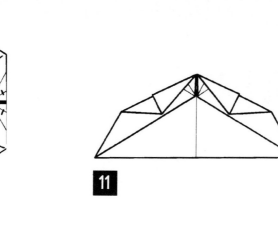

10

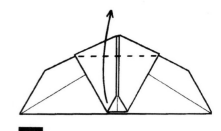

11

12

Step 10

The corners meet the edge.

Step 11 Flip over.

Step 12

Fold this flap up.

Step 13 Flip over.

Step 14

Fold down over the point.

Step 15

Tuck this flap under the other layers.

Step 16 Fold in half.

Step 17 RAT fold.

The finished Invader. Just your typical great Garwood design.

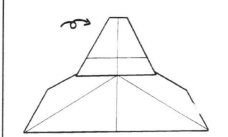

13

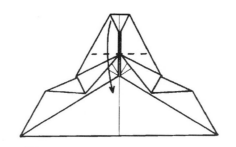

14

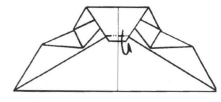

15

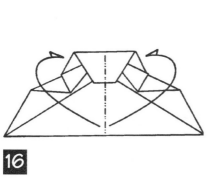

16

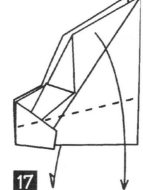

17

Wind Devil II

by Don Garwood

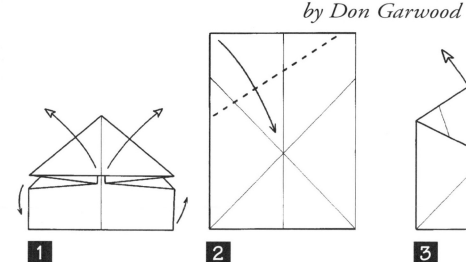

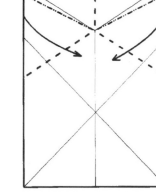

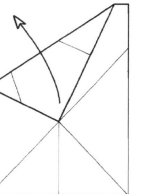

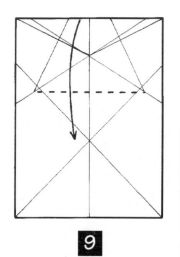

1

2

3

4

5

6

7

8

9

Step 1

Start with a waterbomb base. Unfold and rotate 1/2 turn.

Step 2

This corner goes to the center.

Step 3

Unfold and repeat for the other side.

Step 4

We're going to begin forming a base shown in step 7. Start by following the existing creases for the valley folds. Don't make the mountain folds yet.

Step 5

Now you've got a kind of rabbit ear assembly. Keep moving the raw corners to the center crease.

Step 6

Great! Now squash fold this flap to make the mountain folds back in step 4.

Step 7

The completed base. Fold down along the raw edge.

Step 8

Unfold the whole page.

Step 9

Follow the existing crease as shown.

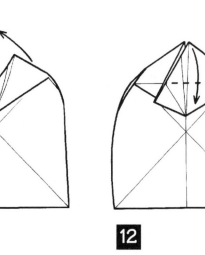

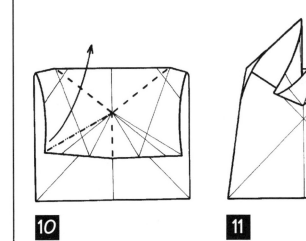

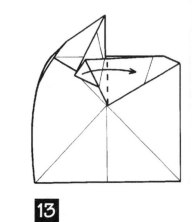

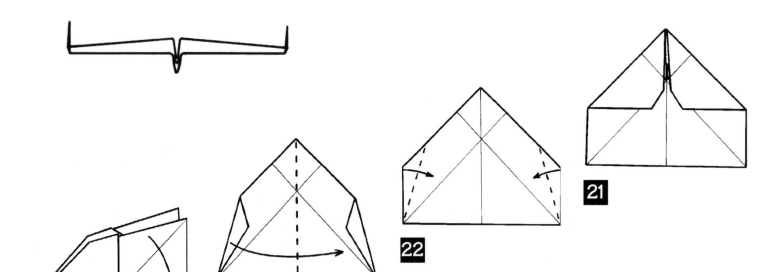

Step 10

We're working with existing creases here. As you move the left corner up, notice the layer on the left won't lay flat. Don't make it lay flat yet.

Step 11

Shows step 10 in progress. Note the layers on either side now not laying flat.

Step 12

Step 10 complete. Fold down along an existing crease.

Step 13

Now that corner lays flat. Fold the flap over to the right.

Step 14

Fold down along the existing crease.

Step 15

Ahhh. Flat again! Lift and squash this flap.

Step 16

Okay weird. Sure, but you got there.

Step 17

A close up view of the carnage. We'll fold these corners behind.

Step 18   The finished fold.

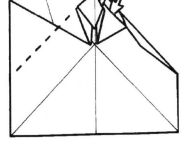

14

15

16

17

18

19

20

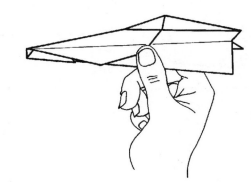

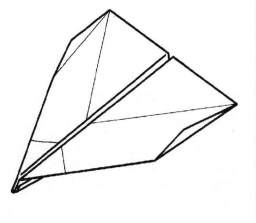

Step 19

Bring the top edges to the center line.

Step 20

You probably spotted the opening on the last move. Now you open the last creases up and put the flaps into the large pockets. This shows the right side going in, but you do both.

Step 21

You're there dude. Flip me over.

Step 22

This is where the winglets will go. Thay likes doing winglets first. I prefer to wait 'til last. He, however, did the drawings.

Step 23   Fold in half.

Step 24

Make the wing fold—a gentle slope up toward the tail. Make the winglets parallel to this crease if you didn't do them in step 22.

There are two ways to go on wing adjustment. First, you could flatten all the creases on the surface and add up elevator. That works o.k… Or, secondly, you can accentuate the front two creases on the surface (mountain near the nose, valley midwing) and flatten the diagonal going toward the rear corners. The second configuration, shown in the photo will give you that amazing wind-vaning effect. The plane will point into the wind and hover, often gaining altitude as it does. Outdoor play is a must.

Outlaw

by Don Garwood

Step 1   Fold in half.

Step 2

Fold the corner to the raw edges.

Step 3   Unfold.

Step 4

Fold the creased edge to the crease.

Step 5

Unfold the whole page.

Step 6

Follow an existing crease.

Step 7

Follow an existing crease.

Step 8

How many times do I have to repeat myself.

Step 9

Just once more I guess.

Step 10

Fold the corners to the center.

Step 11   Flip over.

Step 12   Fold in half.

Step 13

Fold the point back to the top.

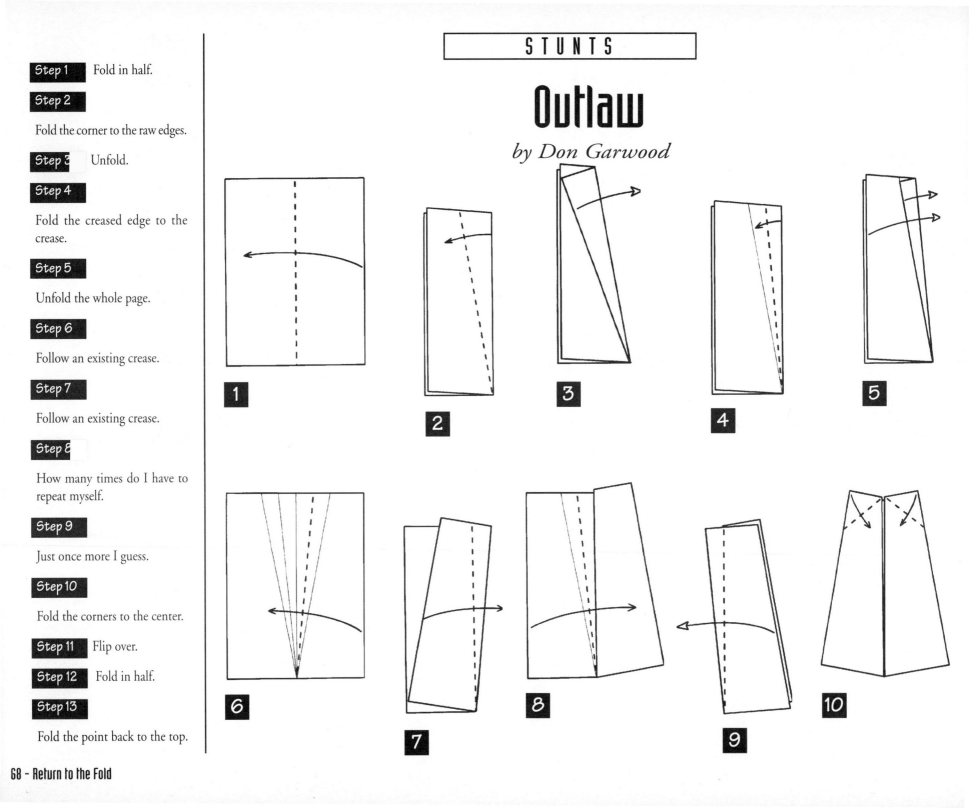

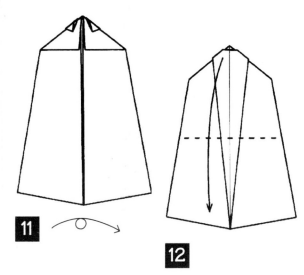

11

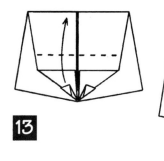

12

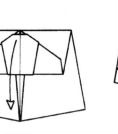

13

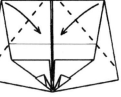

14

15

Step 14 Unfold.

Step 15

Fold the corners to the intersection.

Step 16

A nod to Mr. Nakamura.

Step 17

Fold the flat edge down to meet the bottom of the triangle.

Step 18

Unfold and sink this flap inside.

Step 19

Shows the sink in progress. This is a tough move.

Step 20

A completed sink. Now bend the sink down and:

Step 21

Open up the pocket of the sink and stick the flap inside.

Step 22

You've completed the Outlaw.

The finished Outlaw. Notice the slight curving of the wings. You can play with that. Also note the slight dihedral— almost flat. The Outlaw is a great plane, and as you might expect, it flies where it wants to, on it's own terms.

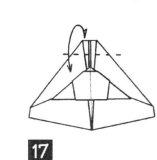

16

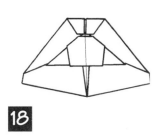

17

18

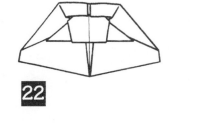

19

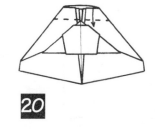

20

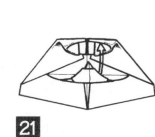

21

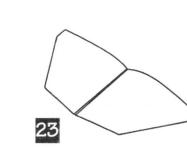

22

23

Gliders

Time aloft is the goal for this group of planes. In the right wind, you'll watch them fly out of sight. Most of them fly exceedingly well outdoors. They have a rare combination of light wing loading, high aspect ration, and strength.

Below: Nakamura Lock, Flatso, LF-2, Flatbed, Mini Flatbed, and LF-1.

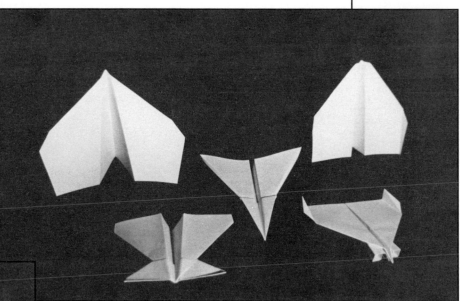

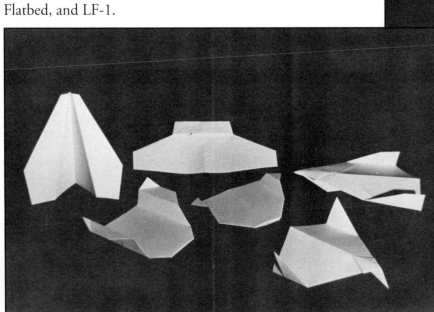

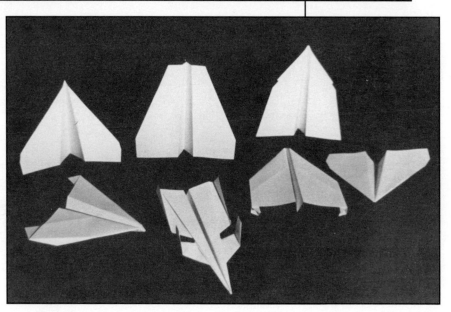

Right: Serge Golian, Blunt Nose, Wild Cat, Phoenix X, Super Canard, Phoenix X with Nacelles, and Cub.

Nakamura Lock

by Nakamura

"You'll find this one of the most pleasing aircraft in this book. It's simple to fold, and it's a great flier. If you only learn one glider from this book, learn this classic, elegant plane. "

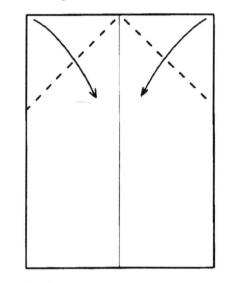

1

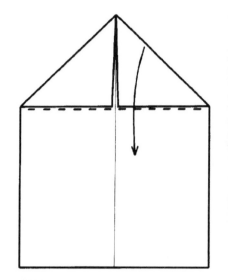

2

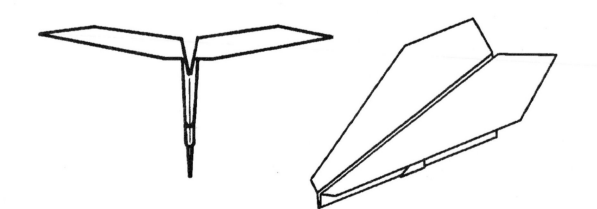

You'll find this one of the most pleasing aircraft in this book. It's simple to fold, and it's a great flier. Don Garwood has cleverly included this elegant locking technique in a number of his designs. If you only learn one glider from this book, learn this classic, elegant plane.

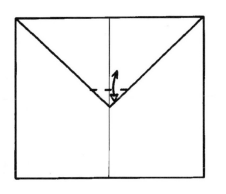

3

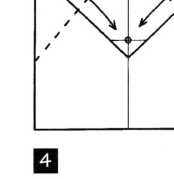

4

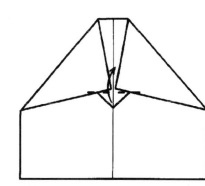

5

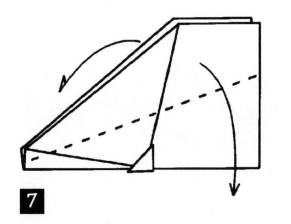

7

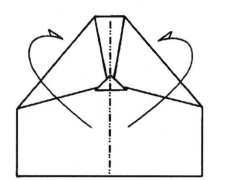

6

After folding in half, bring the corners to the center line.

Step 2

Fold down across the raw edges.

Step 3

Fold up the tip (RAT) a half inch or so and unfold.

Step 4

Bring the corners to the intersection.

Step 5

Fold the flap up. Such a simple move, but it does an incredible thing:

Step 6

Fold the plane in half.

Step 7

Now notice how everything is held together by that tiny locking fold. The glider can't come apart. he creased edge of the wing meets the bottom crease. Notice that the fold starts in the center of the front edge— not in the corner.

The finished Nakamura Lock.

Blunt Nose

by Don Garwood

STEP 1

Start with base #1. Make a pinch in the center of the triangle and then fold the whole triangle down.

STEP 2

Fold the corners to the pinch.

STEP 3

Fold the flap up using the top layers as the limit.

STEP 4

Fold the model in half (mountain fold).

STEP 5

Start the wing crease just shy of half way up the front edge, leave a small corner of the locking flap and end about a quarter way up the back edge.

"This is sort of a Don Garwood-meets-Nakamura design. Of course, Don has designed a terrific flier. It's really this kind of folding economy and elegance you should strive for in creating your designs."

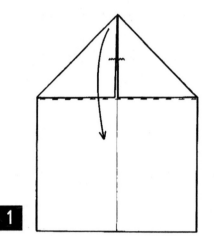

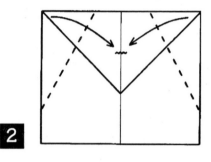

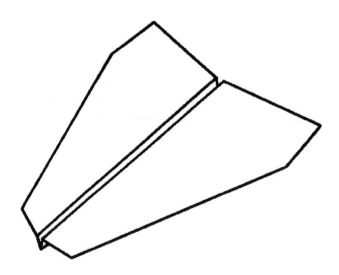

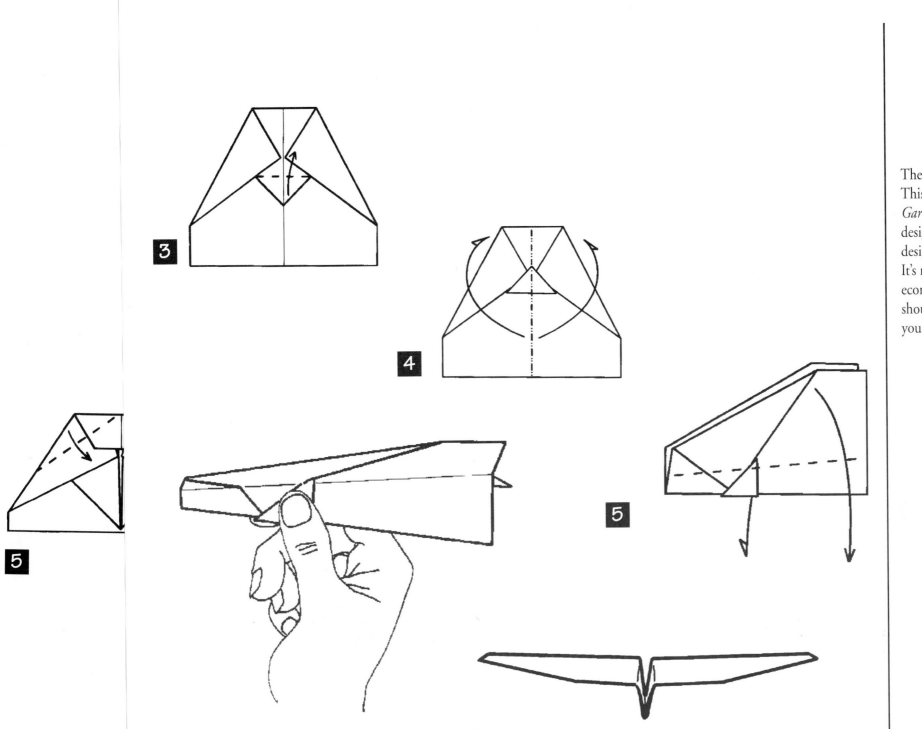

3

4

5

5

5

The finished Blunt nose. This is sort of a *Don Garwood-meets-Nakamura* design. Of course, Don has designed a terrific flier. It's really this kind of folding economy and elegance you should strive for in creating your designs.

Serge Golian

by Don Garwood

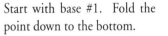

Step 1

Start with base #1.

Step 2

Bring the top to th

Step 3

Mark the center of
with a pinch. The
corners to the pinch

Step 4

Fold the top down al
edges underneath.

Step 5

Fold the corners to
edge.

Step 1

Start with base #1. Fold the point down to the bottom.

Step 2

Make a pinch fold at the half way mark and then bring the corners to the pinch.

Step 3 Unfold.

Step 4

Bring the raw edges to the new crease.

Step 5

Now bring the new corners to the pinch.

Step 6

Bring the flap up, making a Nakamura type lock.

Step 7

Fold the plane in half.

Step 8

Start close to the nose to make the wing crease and end just a little shy of half way up the back edge. You can vary this wing crease quite a bit. Don suggests you try a wide variety of folds.

The finished Serge Golian.

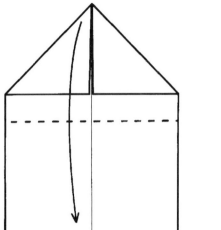

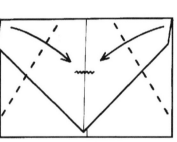

1

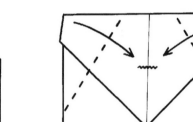

2

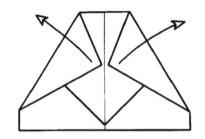

3

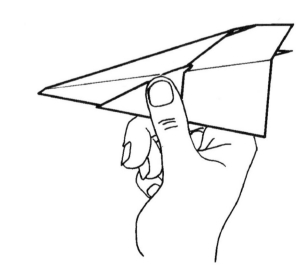

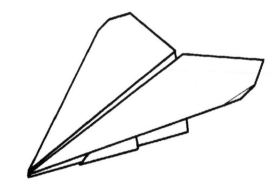

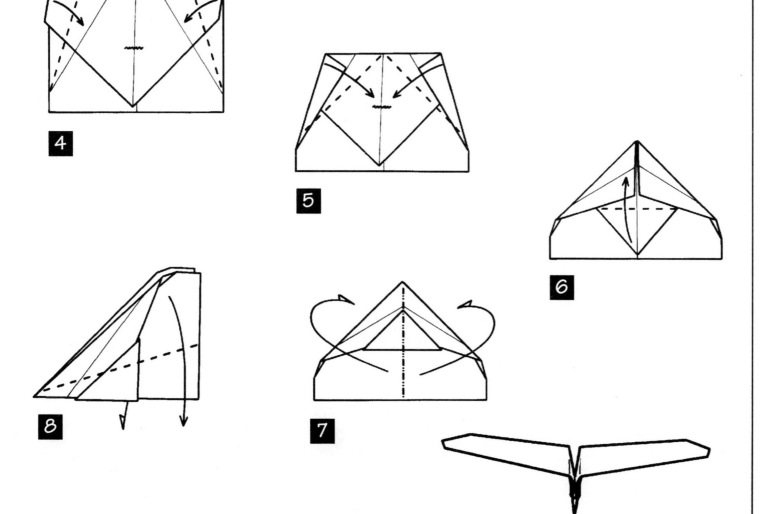

4

5

6

8

7

Serge was an engineer in the space program and a friend of Don's. They shared music and other good times together. It must have been a gas just hanging around Mr. Golian long enough for some smarty pants to say to him, "What are you, a rocket scientist?" Which, of course, Serge could answer, "As a matter of fact, Yes. Here's my card."

Phoenix X

by John M. Collins

Step 1

Book fold and unfold.

Step 2

Fold the corner to the bottom.

Step 3

Unfold and repeat for the other side.

Step 4

Place the raw edge against the crease and make the fold.

Step 5

Repeat for the left side. You can line up the corner with the end of the marked crease to help guide the fold.

Step 6

Rotate 1/2 turn.

Step 7

Fold down along the crease.

Step 8

The corners go to the center.

Step 9

Fold the flap up, locking the layers in place.

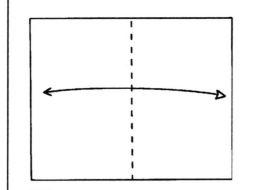

1

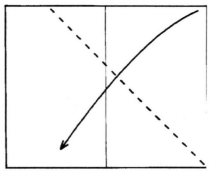

2

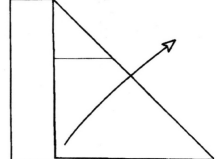

3

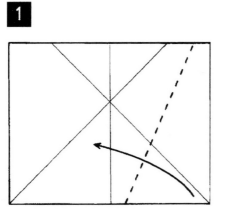

4

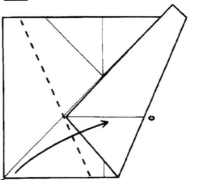

5

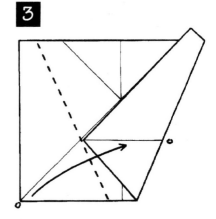

6

7

8

9

The crosswise folding at the start gives you the advantage of more wing span for this glider. Careful in high winds. This one will head for the hills.

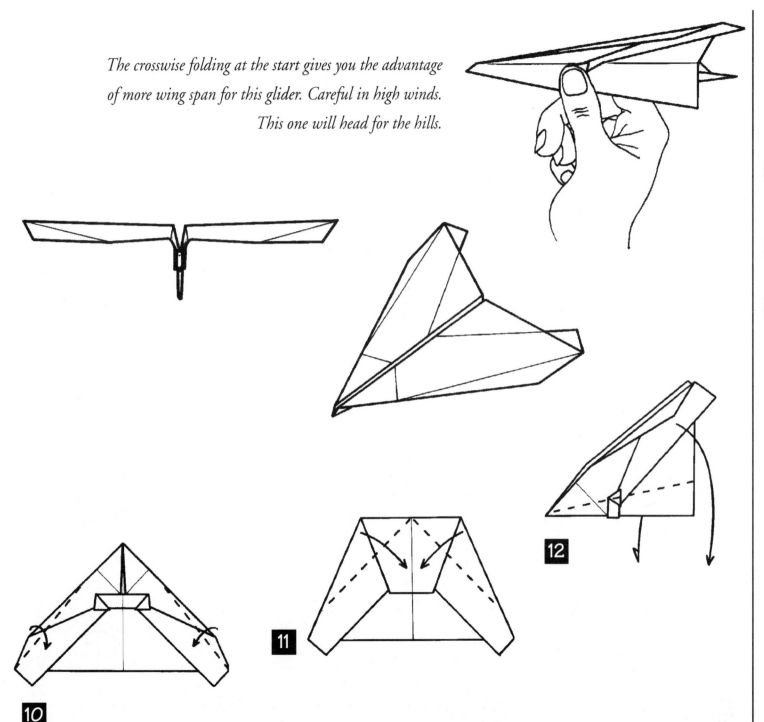

Step 10

Make a wingtip washout fold on each wing.

Step 11

Fold in half.

Step 12

Make the wing fold start at the nose and cross the locking fold where shown.

The finished Phoenix X. The crosswise folding at the start gives you the advantage of more wing span for this glider. Careful in high winds. This one will head for the hills.

Pheonix X with Nacelles

by John M. Collins

Step 1

Book fold and unfold. Make a diagonal corner to corner.

Step 2

Unfold and repeat for the other side.

Step 3

Fold the top to the center.

Step 4   Unfold.

Step 5

Make these folds by putting the ends of the crease directly on the center point.

Step 6

Fold the top edge to the intersection.

Step 7

The top creased edge lines up with the center line.

Step 8

The nacelles start to get formed here. Make creases that start where the raw edges meet and extend to the corners shown. For best results cut into the corners a little.

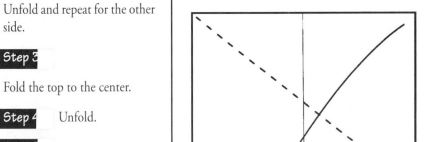

1

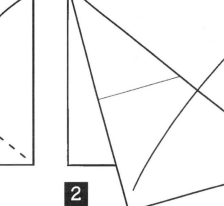

2

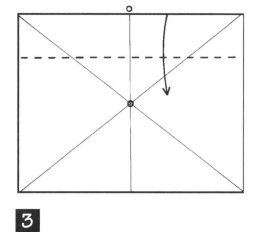

3

4

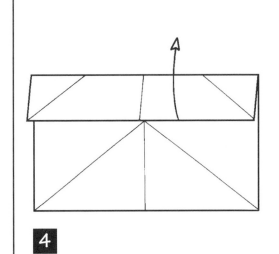

5

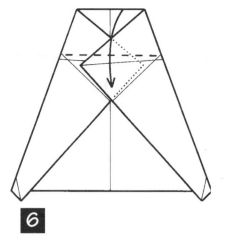

6

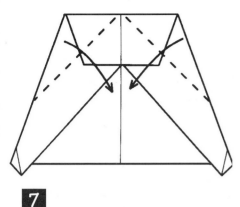

7

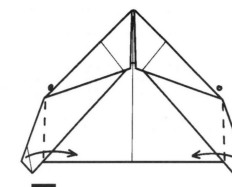

8

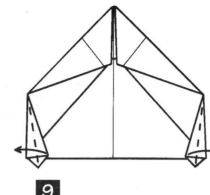

9

Step 9

Fold the creased edge to meet creased edge.

Step 10

Lift and squash.

Step 11

Another view of the squash happening.

Step 12

The nacelles formed, now make wing creases. RAT fold as shown.

The completed Phoenix X with Nacelles. A smooth addition to any glider collection. Great indoors or out, and aesthetically pleasing.

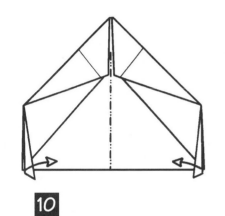

10

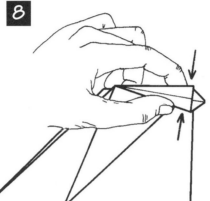

11

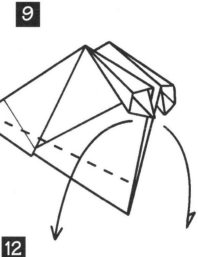

12

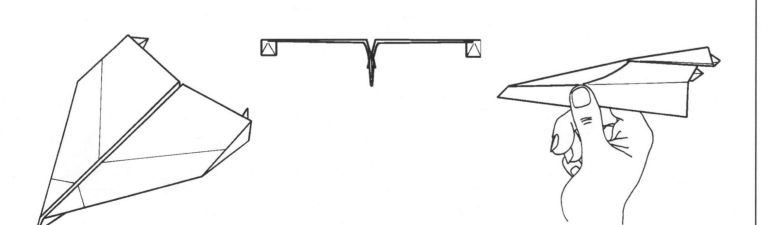

LF - 1

by John M. Collins

Step 1

Fold the page in half.

Step 2

Fold across the diagonal.

Step 3 Unfold.

Step 4

The raw edge rests on the crease.

Step 5

Refold the crease.

Step 6

Locate the halfway point in the base and fold the nose corner straight up.

Step 7

Unfold and reverse.

Step 8

Shows the model opening up in preparation for the reverse.

Step 9

The completed reverse. Now fold the wing down from one corner to the other.

Step 10

Squash fold this point.

Step 11

The squash is happening.

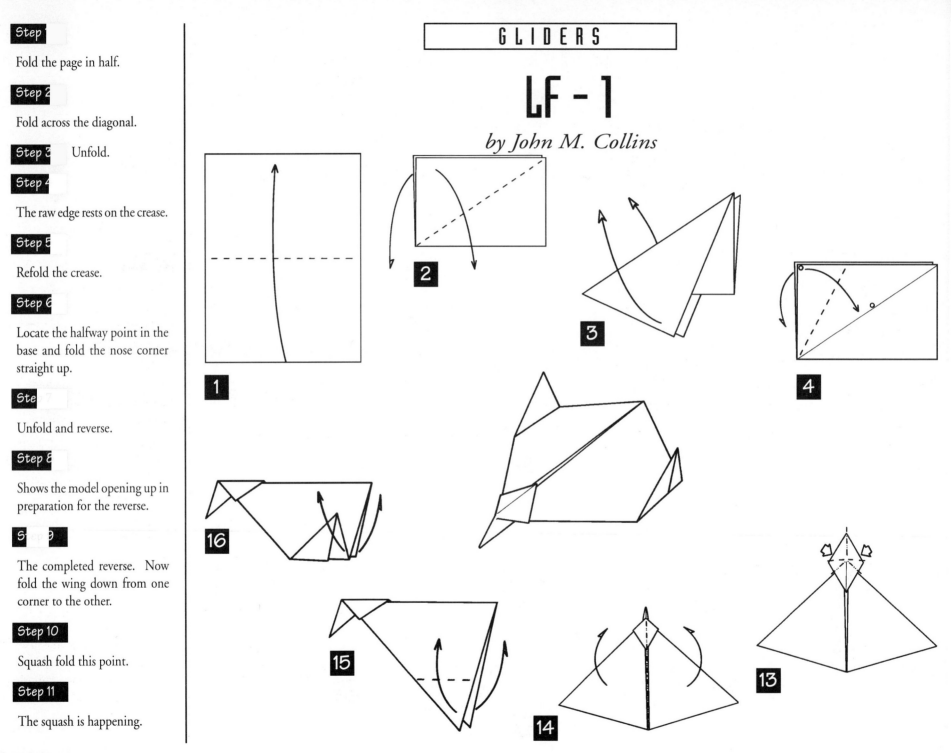

Notice the negative dihedral or anhedral angle. This can be a little fussy to trim. You should be able to get some awesome, smooth glides indoors, and some wild outdoor flights.

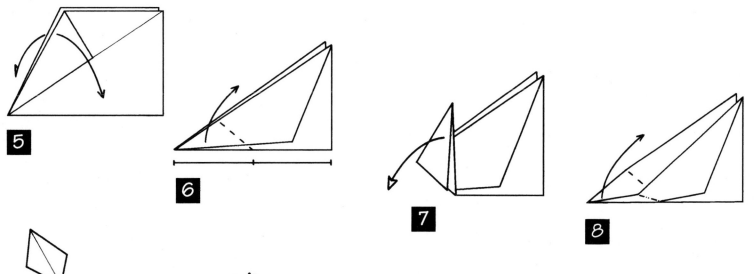

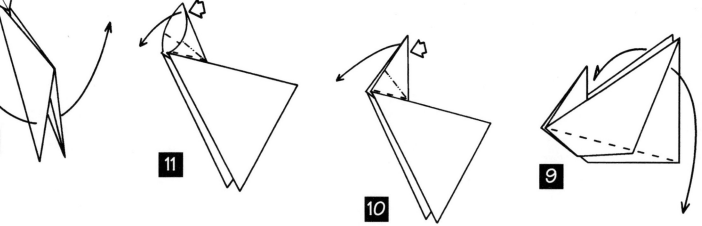

Step 12

The completed squash. Now bring the wings up and lay the model out flat.

Step 13

This is a rabbit ear sort of move. Follow the edge of the wings, and just wrap the paper around.

Step 14

Now remake the wing folds—keep the nose layers together. They'll be getting creased here too.

Step 15

Fold parallel to the wing crease, a bit less than a third.

Step 16

And open up.

The finished LF-1. Notice the negative dihedral or anhedral angle. This can be a little fussy to trim. You should be able to get some awesome, smooth glides indoors, and some wild outdoor flights.

LF-2

by John M. Collins

Step 1

Fold in half.

Step 2

Fold the corners down.

Step 3

Fold the triangle in half.

Step 4

Unfold and then reverse the point.

Step 5

Fold down from one corner to the other.

Step 6

Fold the corner up to the creased edge.

The finished LF-2. The LF or Locked Fuselage designs both have negative dihedral. It's important to keep the winglet vertical. You should get smooth, straight glides from this one indoors. Sudden gusts of wind may cause barrel rolling outdoors.

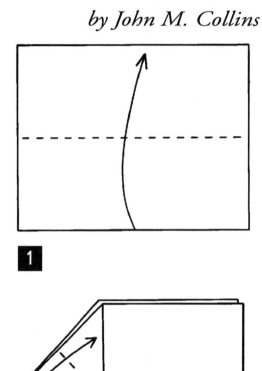

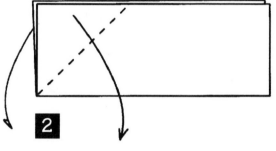

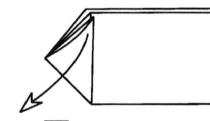

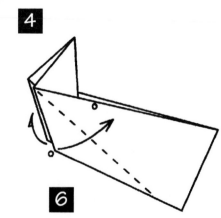

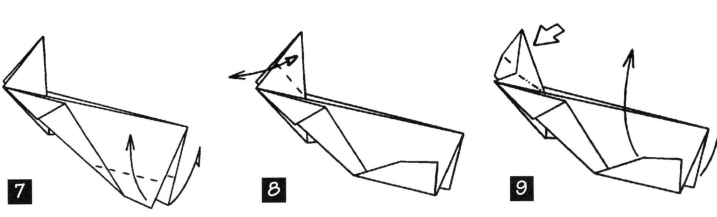

7

8

9

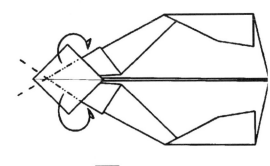

10

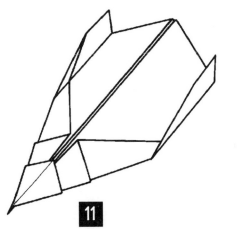

11

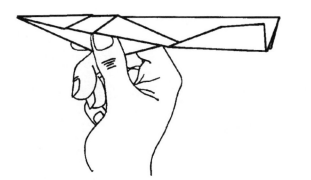

Step 7

Make winglets— about one third the available width.

Step 8

Fold, unfold and Squash this point.

Step 9

The Squash happening. Pull the wings up and flatten the model.

Step 10

A rabbit ear kind of move happens here. Just wrap the layers around the edge of the wing and bring it all together underneath. Remake the wing creases to lock it all in.

Step 11

Just open it up.

Slo-Mo

by John M. Collins

STEP 1

Fold in half.

STEP 2

Fold the corner down and repeat for the other side.

STEP 3

Fold the raw edge under to the crease from step 2. It's easier if you unfold to step 2, fold the edge to the crease, and the remake the step 2 fold. After making the creases, open the model up.

STEP 4

Fold the nose down until it extends about one half inch beyond where the layers come together. It's a RAT fold.

STEP 5

Starting at the center of the model, fold the two corners down to the creased edge.

STEP 6

Mountain fold in half.

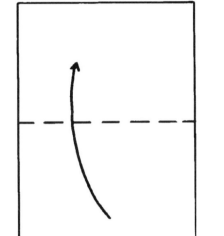

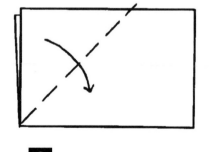

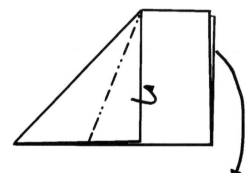

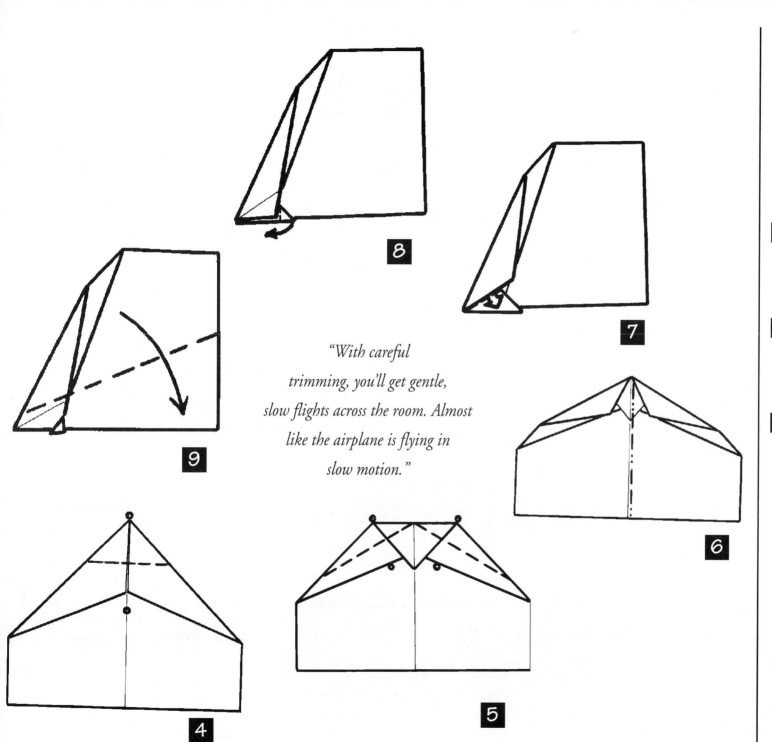

"With careful trimming, you'll get gentle, slow flights across the room. Almost like the airplane is flying in slow motion."

STEP 7

Pull down the inside layers by making a valley fold on the layer shown. Repeat for the other side.

STEP 8

Open the model up enough to fold the triangle back over the other layers.

STEP 9

Make a wing fold starting close to the nose and sloping up toward the tail. The creases should end at about the center of the raw edge.

The finished Slo-Mo. This airplane was invented for minimum wing loading. It was an attempt at developing the Folded Follow Foil. It did eventually lead to that elusive airplane. But with careful trimming, you'll get gentle, slow flights across the room. Almost like the airplane is flying in slow motion.

Whip it

by John M. Collins

STEP 1

Start with a waterbomb base. Fold the point down to the top raw edge.

STEP 2

Using the crease from step 1, lift the top layer of the waterbomb base. Don't make a new crease yet.

STEP 3

Make two valley folds by moving the point over to the creased edge. Notice that the point extends past the center.

STEP 4

Do the same to the left side.

STEP 5

To make this fold, I usually place my thumbs between the layers where the large arrows are. Lift the two flaps shown by the small arrows and squash fold them by making the valley folds as shown.

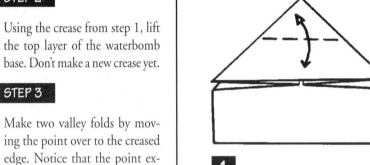

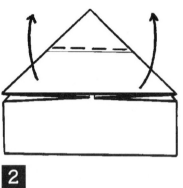

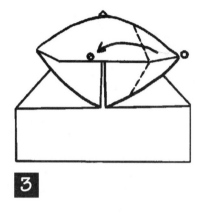

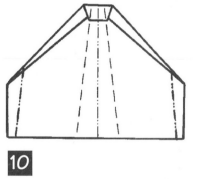

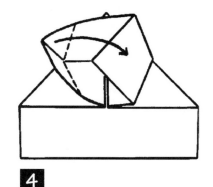

4

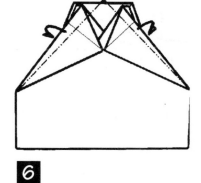

5

"A very sturdy, all purpose glider. High winds outdoors—no problem. Need a fast strafing run indoors —no sweat."

6

8

9

7

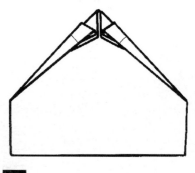

STEP 6

Fold all the layers back along the edge of the original waterbomb shape. Then flip the model over.

STEP 7

The flipped over model.

STEP 8

Fold the nose down and pull the top layers apart by making a valley and mountain on each.

STEP 9

The finished fold from step 8.

STEP 10

Make the fuselage and wing folds. Then make the winglet folds parallel to the wing folds.

The finished Whip It. A very sturdy, all purpose glider. High winds outdoors—no problem. Need a fast strafing run indoors—no sweat. You may need a touch of up elevator.

Flatbed

by John M. Collins

Step 1

The classic waterbomb base. The points go to the top.

Step 2

The creased edges go to the center.

Step 3

The top triangle comes down over the creased edges.

Step 4

Now open up the three points in order to:

Step 5

Put the outside corners into the pockets.

Step 6

This is an old, classic nose weighting system. All kinds of wing forms are possible after making this part of the plane. Flip over.

Step 7

Fold the raw edges to the center.

Step 8

Fold the raw edges to the creased edges.

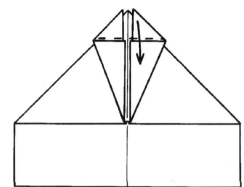

3

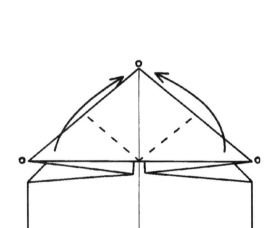

1

2

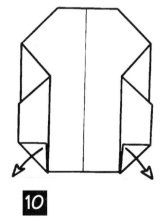

10

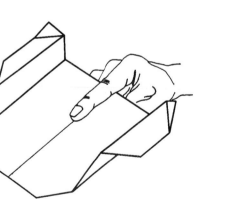

You can grip the triangular weighting system underneath or throw as the diagram shows. Either way, this is a tremendous outdoor glider, particularly in high wind.

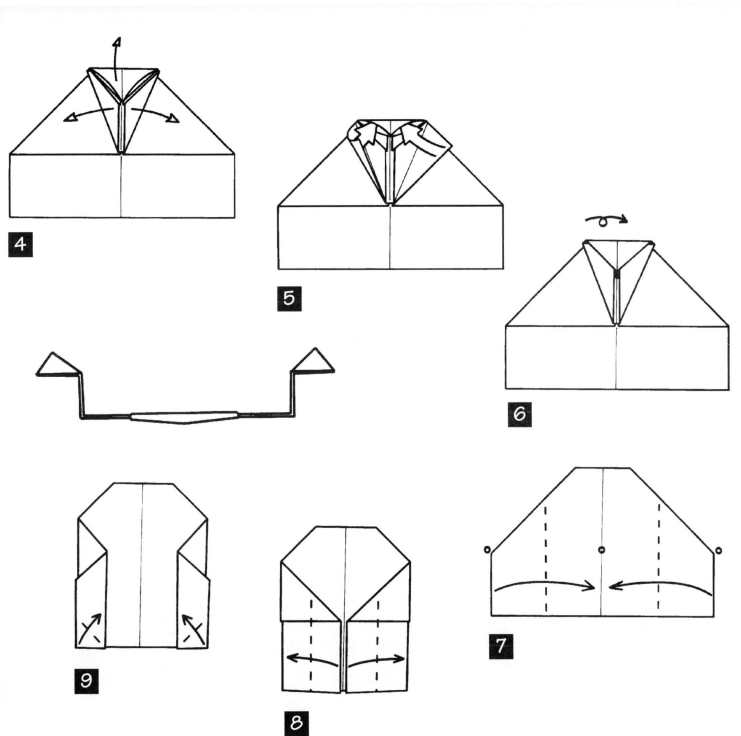

Make up elevator creases.

Step 10

Open up the wing creases.

The finished Flatbed. This was one of the first gliders I played with as a young boy. It was my mother who had learned to make the waterbomb base and taught it to me and my six brothers. Maybe it was just a shrewd move to get us out of the house. You can grip the triangular weighting system underneath or throw as the diagram shows. Either way, this is a tremendous outdoor glider, particularly in high wind.

Mini Flatbed
by John M. Collins

Book fold and then fold the outside edges to the center.

Step 2

Fold these corners out.

Step 3

This is really a diagonal fold. Line up the top raw edge with the creased edge on the left.

Step 4

Unfold and repeat for the other side.

Step 5

Make a mountain fold across the intersection and then waterbomb.

These points go up like an origami cup.

Step 7 Unfold.

Step 8

The point gets folded down across the ends of the creases.

Step 9

Remake these creases, only this time:

Step 10

Put one flap inside the other.

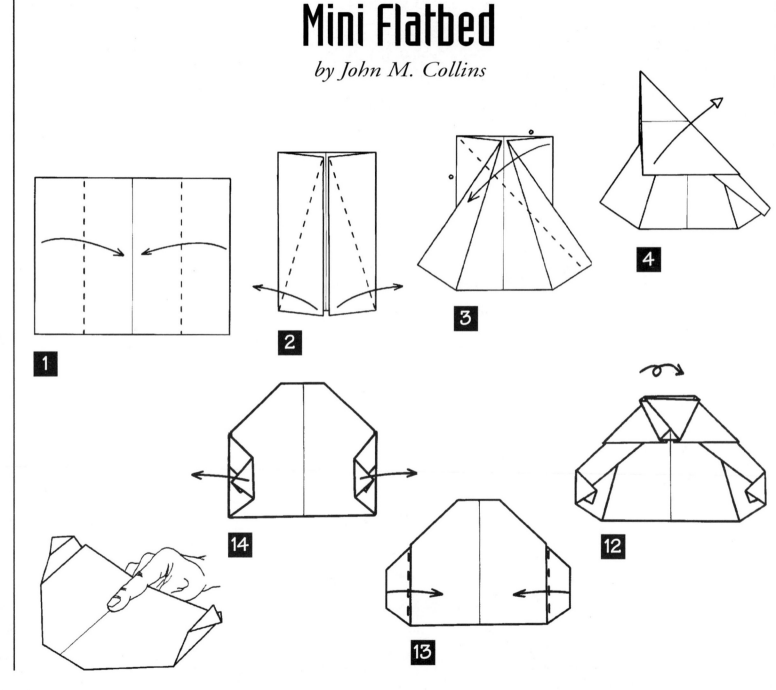

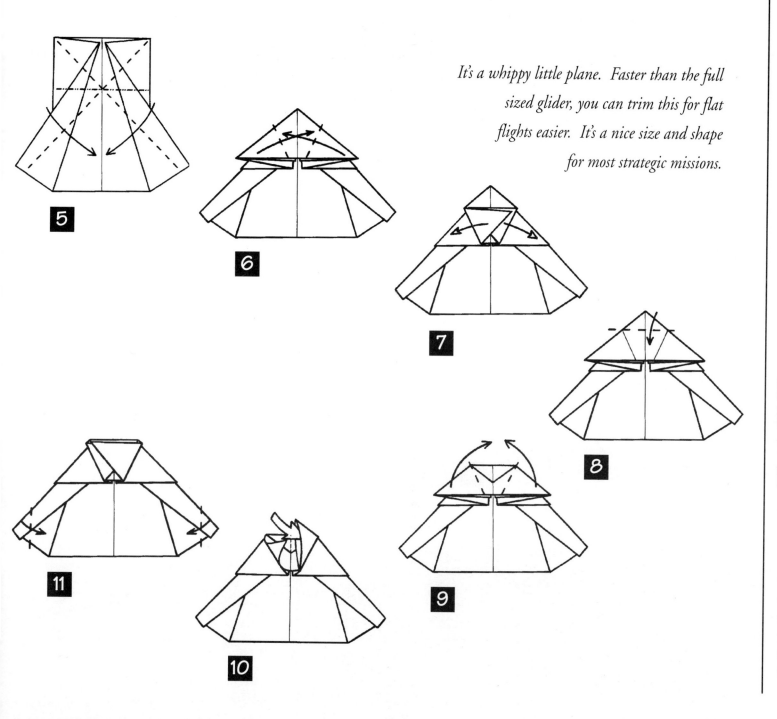

It's a whippy little plane. Faster than the full sized glider, you can trim this for flat flights easier. It's a nice size and shape for most strategic missions.

Step 11

These winglet folds are parallel with the center crease. The points will just touch the vertical creased edge position on the other side of the model.

Step 12   Flip over.

Step 13

Fold along the creased edge.

Step 14

Open up the wing folds so that they are vertical and horizontal.

The finished Mini Flatbed. It's a whippy little plane. Faster than the full sized glider, you can trim this for flat flights easier. It's a nice size and shape for most strategic missions.

Flatso

by Don Garwood

Step 1

Book fold and pinch the center of the crease. The bring the corners to that pinch.

Step 2

Bring the small raw edges to the center. Be careful to make your crease parallel with the creased edge.

Step 3

Mountain fold across the center pinch.

Step 4

This fold starts at the center and then goes to the outside corner. (both sides)

Step 5   Flip over.

Step 6

This is a complex move. The valley fold happens on the back layer. We pull open this pocket, lift it upward, and then squash it flat. Step 7 shows how to start.

Step 7

We're opening the pocket—now lift and squash.

Step 8

The finished fold. Flip over.

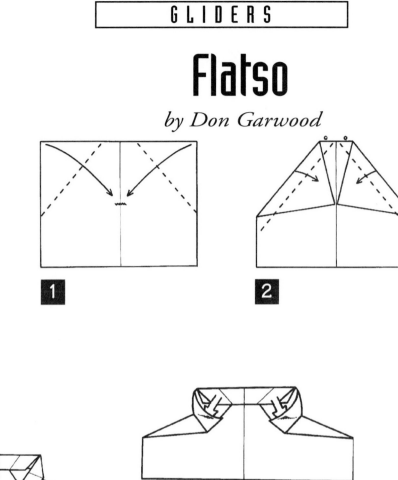

1

2

3

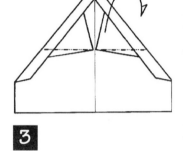

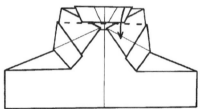

10

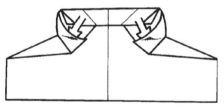

11

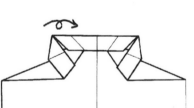

12

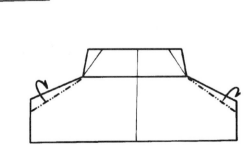

13

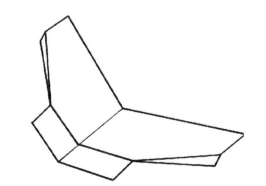

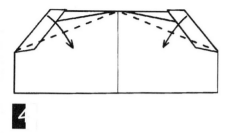

4

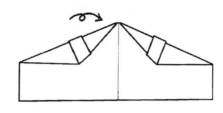

5

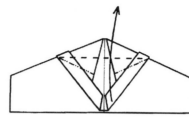

6

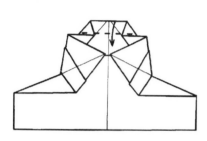

9

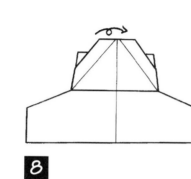

8

7

Step 9

Fold the small flap over.

Step 10

Fold the larger flap over.

Step 11

And tuck the corners into the pockets.

Step 12 Flip over.

Step 13

Make a leading edge washout fold. This really helps stabilize the glider.

The finished Flatso. It's hard to find a glider with a better glide ratio. This thing loses almost no altitude going across the average living room. The Flatso tends to be a little squirrely outside. Another amazing Garwood design.

It's hard to find a glider with a better glide ratio. This thing loses almost no altitude going across the average living room. The Flatso tends to be a little squirrely outside. Another amazing Garwood design.

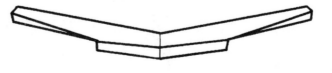

Wild Cat

by Don Garwood

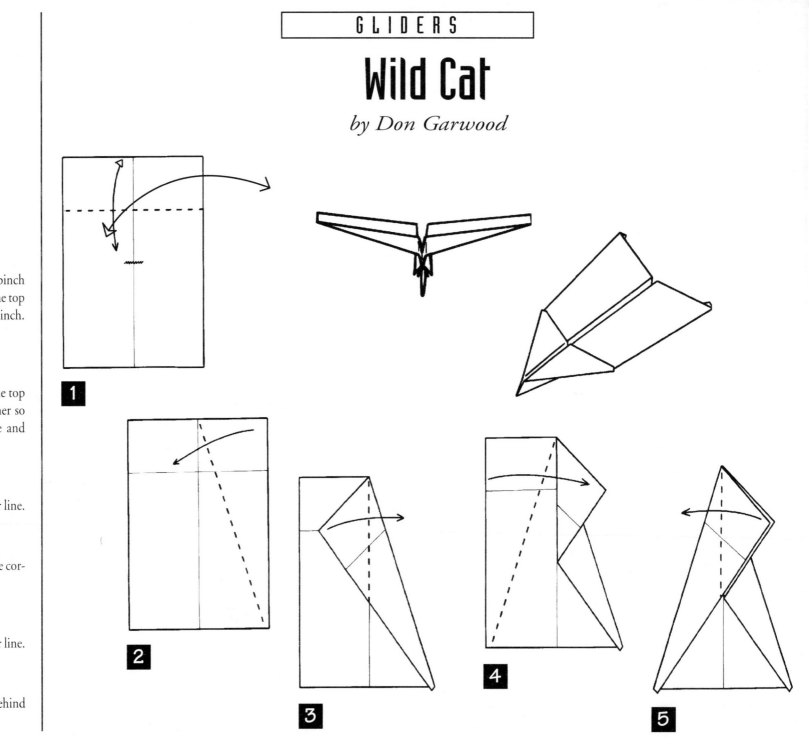

Step 1

Fold in half and make a pinch mark in the center. Fold the top edge down to meet the pinch. Unfold.

Step 2

Starting at the center of the top edge, move the right corner so that it touches the crease and make the fold.

Step 3

Fold back along the center line.

Step 4

Fold the left side over. The corners should match up.

Step 5

Fold back along the center line.

Step 6

Mountain fold the top behind where shown.

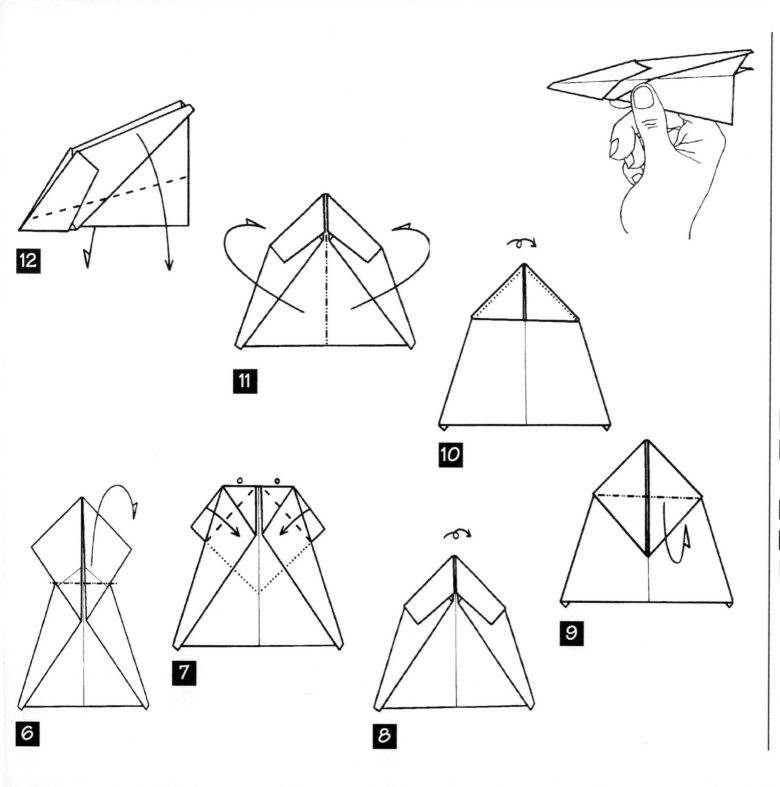

Another clean design by Don Garwood. Accurate, graceful, and great indoors or out.

Step 7

Fold the marked edges to the center. (dots show the layer behind)

Step 8 Flip over.

Step 9

Fold this whole flap to the inside.

Step 10 Flip over.

Step 11 Fold in half.

Step 12

The wing fold start close to the nose and ends just short of half way up the rear edge.

The finished Wildcat. Another clean design by Don Garwood. Accurate, graceful, and great indoors or out.

12

11

10

9

8

7

6

Twin Nacelle
by John M. Collins

Step 1

Fold in half along the length and width.

Step 2

Move the corner to the raw edge at the end of the crease. Start the crease here at the raw edge. You only need to make a partial crease— stop when you hit the other crease. You'll do this move to all four corners. These creases allow you to make the folds in step 3.

Step 3

Reverse the corners— the right one is happening.

Step 4   Now the left.

Step 5

Move the right flap all the way to the left. The layers underneath will be your limit.

Step 6

Unfold and do the same for the other side.

Step 7

Follow just the upper part of the valleys.

Step 8

Bring them together like so, and mountain fold the center crease.

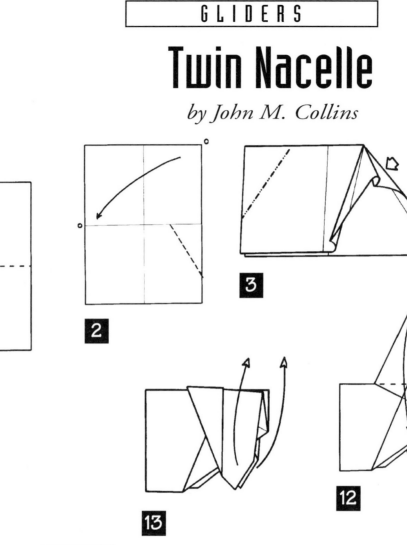

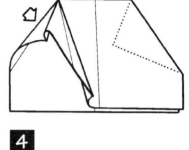

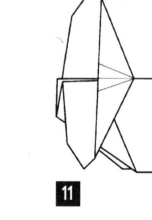

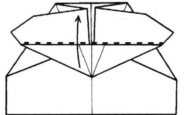

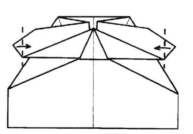

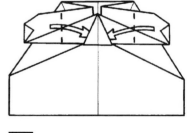

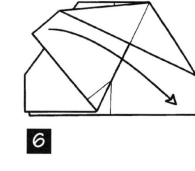

6

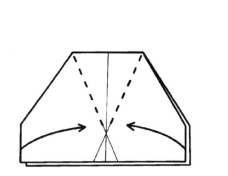

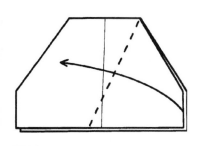

5

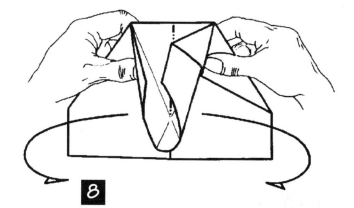

7

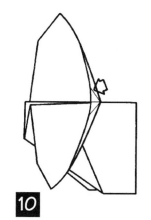

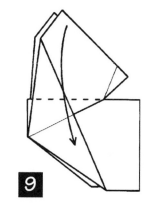

9

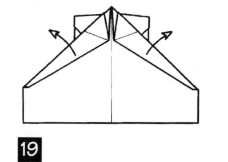

8

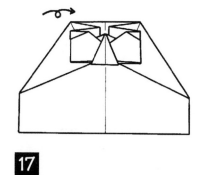

10

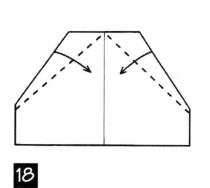

17

18

19

Step 9

Bring the top flap down and make a sqaush. Step 10 shows the sqash happening.

Step 10

The squash in action.

Step 11

The finished squash. Flip over.

Step 12

Bring this flap down.

Step 13

Flatten the center crease again.

Step 14

Fold the triangle up.

Step 15

Square off the tips.

Step 16

Insert the flaps into the triangle pockets. Make a sharp crease.

Step 17 Flip over.

Step 18

Fold the top edges to the center line.

Step 19 Unfold.

Step 20

Turn the creases into mountain folds, tucking them under the layers on the other side.

Step 21

Fold the plane in half.

Step 22

Fold the marked corners together. Flip over and do the other side.

Step 23

Make the wing crease parallel to the center crease and go right across the tip of the triangle.

Step 24

Now open up the nacelles by squashing them open. You may want to use a pencil to help open them up.

Step 25

A close up detail of the winglets being formed. Make sure they match.

The finished Twin Nacelle. You'll need to add some up elevator to get the smooth, level flights this glider is capable of. It's very sturdy and aesthetically pleasing. Great indoors or out.

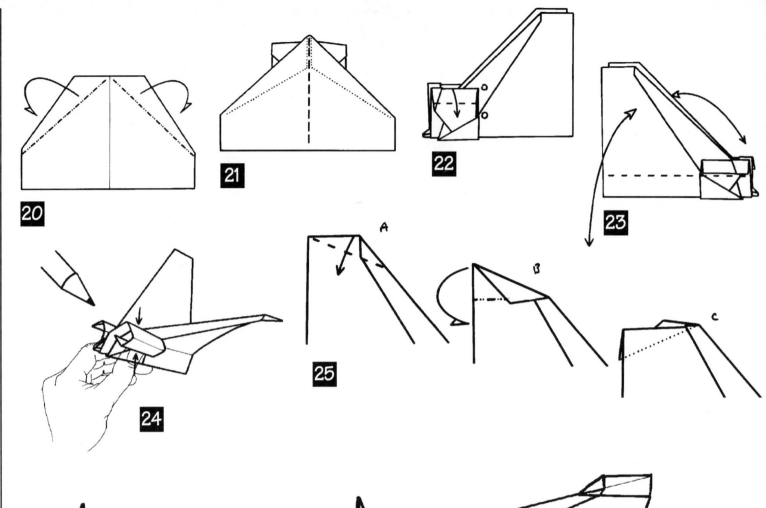

Needle Nose

by Don Garwood

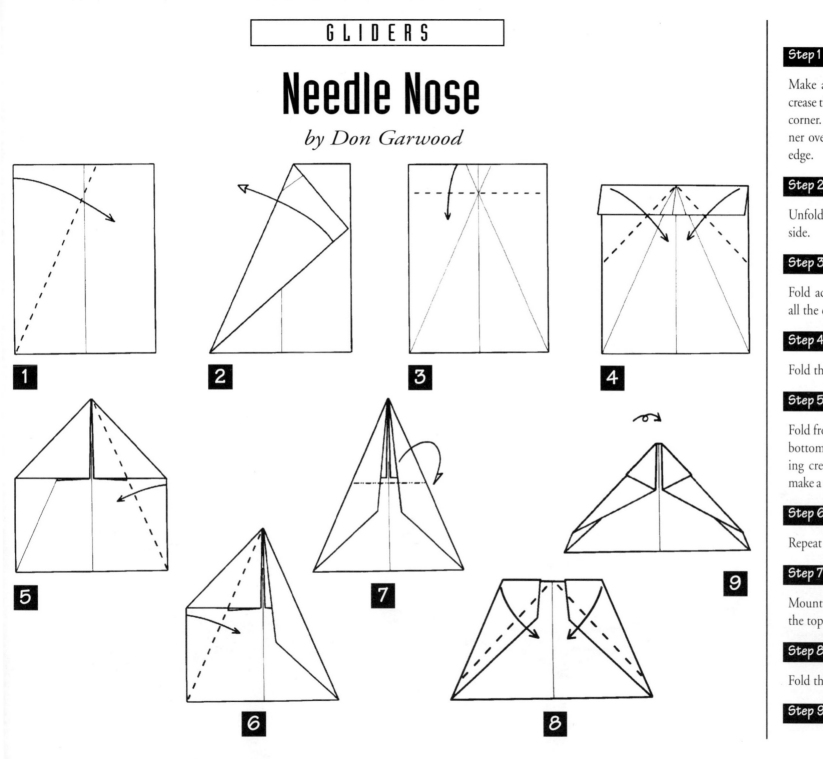

Step 1

Make a center crease. Make a crease that starts at the lower left corner. Bring the upper left corner over to meet the right raw edge.

Step 2

Unfold and repeat for the other side.

Step 3

Fold across the intersection of all the creases.

Step 4

Fold the corners to the center.

Step 5

Fold from the top corner to the bottom right. Follow the existing crease where you can and make a new one on the top layer.

Step 6

Repeat for the left side.

Step 7

Mountain fold in half, folding the top back.

Step 8

Fold the corners to the center.

Step 9 Flip over.

Step 10

Fold the flap up as far as possible.

Step 11

Fold the model in half.

Step 12

Make a wing fold that brings the front creased edge to the base and continues to the rear.

Step 13

You may want to add a leading edge fold for extra stability. Otherwise you're finished.

The Needle Nose is a Leading Edge Extension Delta Wing aircraft. NASA folks like the characteristics of this shape so much they put a version of it on the space shuttle.

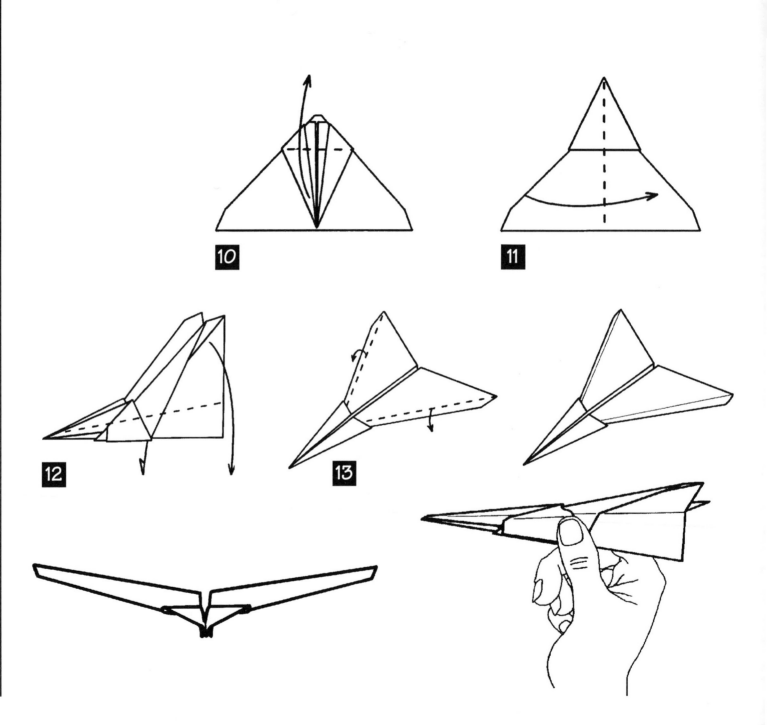

Hammerhead

by Don Garwood

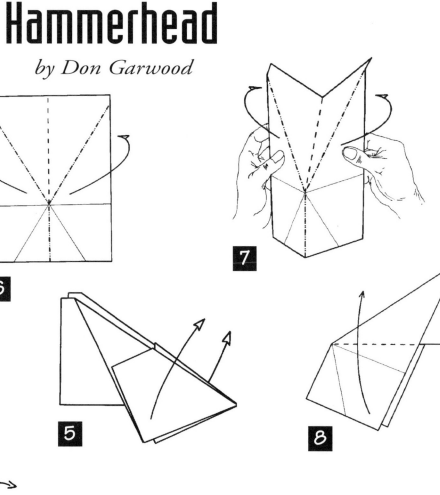

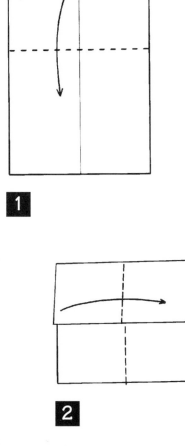

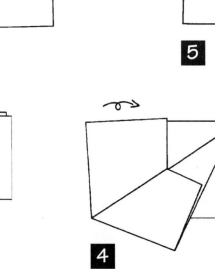

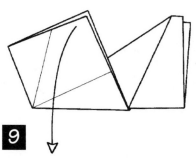

After folding in half along the length, fold the top down about one third. You can easily judge one third by making the layered part the same width as the unlayered part.

Step 2 Fold in half.

Step 3

Fold this corner down leaving about 1/2 to 3/4 inch of raw edge at the rear.

Step 4

Flip over and repeat for the other side.

Step 5

Unfold the whole model.

Step 6

Follow existing creases to make a giant reverse fold.

Step 7

The reverse fold happening.

Step 8

The completed fold. Fold this whole flap up, lining it up with the center crease.

Step 9

Unfold and and open up the paper again.

Step 10

Now using existing creases, press together a waterbomb-like base.

Step 11

Fold the top down to the other points.

Step 12
Unfold.

Step 13

Mountain fold the top back along the existing crease.

Step 14

Unfold the whole paper again.

Step 15

Now we're making a squared off waterbomb-like base.

Step 16

It's coming together.

Step 17

The completed base. Now we'll make a waterbomb-like fold on the top layers.

Step 18

The move in progress. The mountain fold get pushed to the center.

Step 19

And the raw edge goes up.

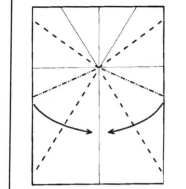

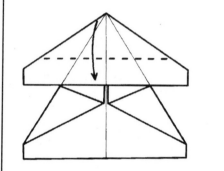

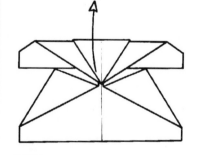

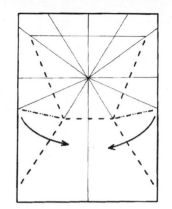

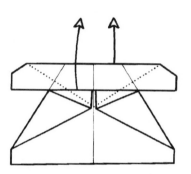

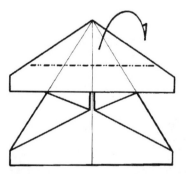

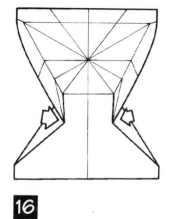

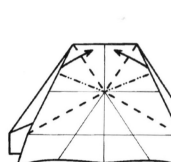

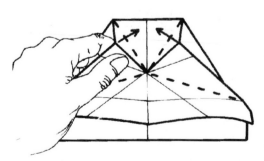

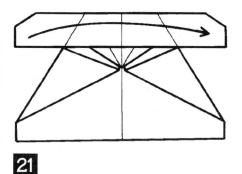

21

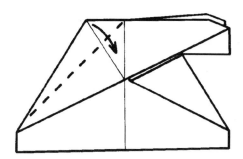

22

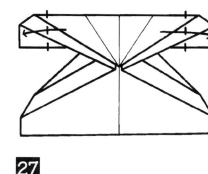

27

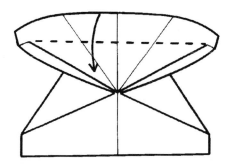

20

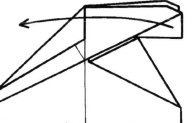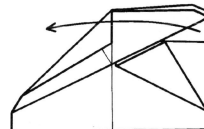

23

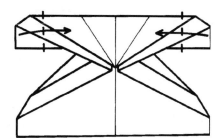

26

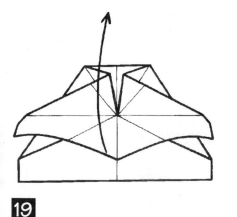

19

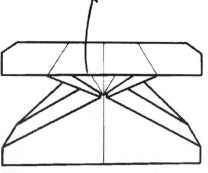

24

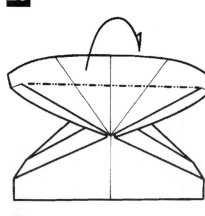

25

Reverse fold. Again, the corners will smush (there's a technical term for you). Don't worry.

Step 29 Fold in half.

Step 30

Tuck this whole flap inside and repeat for the other side.

Step 31

Make the wing fold as shown. You can RAT fold it or follow the measurements.

Step 32

Make leading edge folds to the canards. You can control climbing and turning by adjusting together or asymmetrically.

The finished Hammerhead. One of the few true canard designs in the paper glider realm. The difficult folding is well worth the fun and challenge of learning to control the unique craft. Like most Garwood designs, the Hammerhead is locked together very well, so give this a try in extreme conditions.

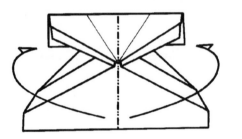

28

29

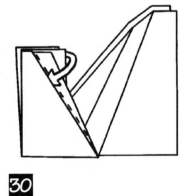

30

31

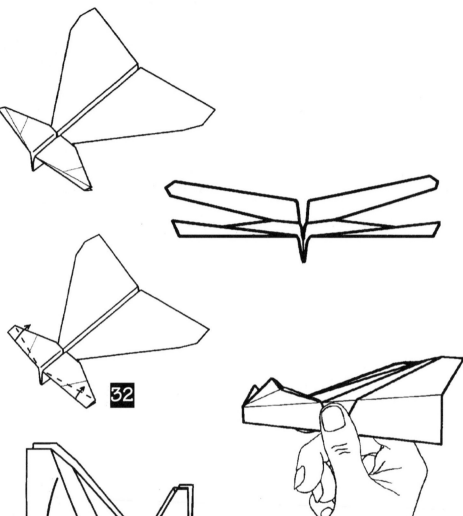

32

GLIDERS

Super Canard
by John M. Collins

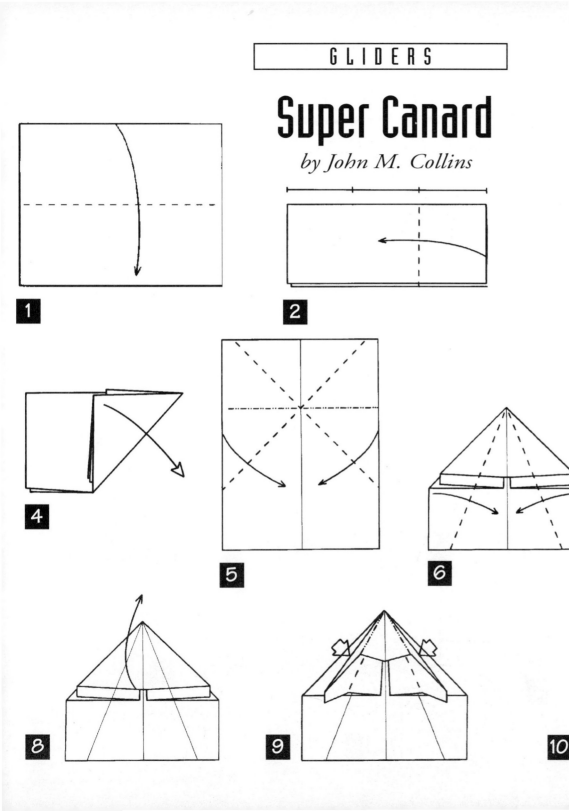

Step 1 Fold in half.

Step 2

Fold over 1/3— the layered part will be the same size as the unlayered part.

Step 3

Fold This corner up to the creased edges. Line it up carefully. The layers will tend to slip and slide around.

Step 4

Unfold and open up the page.

Step 5

Waterbomb it using existing creases.

Step 6

On each side, fold both flaps to the center.

Step 7 Unfold.

Step 8

Lift this layer slightly in preparation for reversing the top flaps.

Step 9

Here we go. Reverse fold these flaps.

Step 10

Now lift this assembly to begin reversing the back flaps.

Step 11

Push in here to reverse the creases.

Step 12

It all presses flat to look like this. Now a petal fold.

Step 13

The petal in progress.

Step 14

The complete petal. Now we'll begin the process of moving this petal point underneath the other layers of the petal.

Unfold the petal.

Step 15

Now tuck the point to the inside as you remake the creases. 16 shows how to start

Step 16

Open this section up, and bend the raw edges to the inside.

Step 17

You did it. This is a weird little move: pull the top right flap to the left while lifting the center layer to the left as well.

Step 18

Severe weirdness is about to occur. You're going to sort of reverse fold this flap up and to the right. The diagonal valley folds

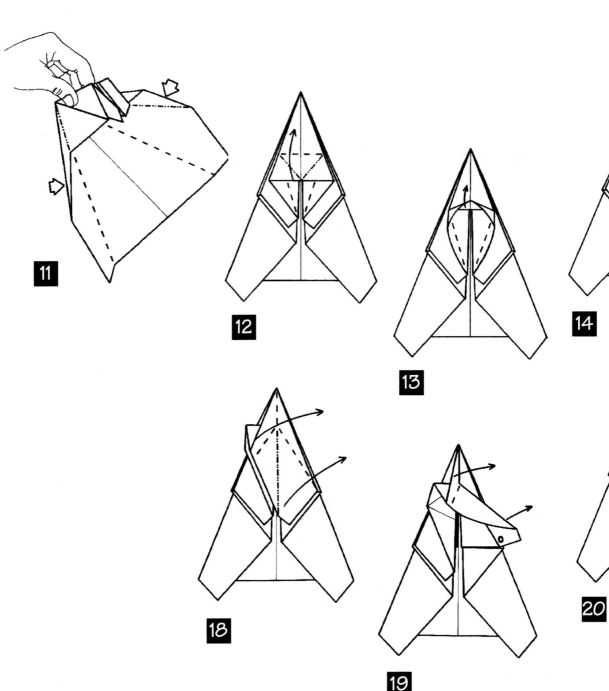

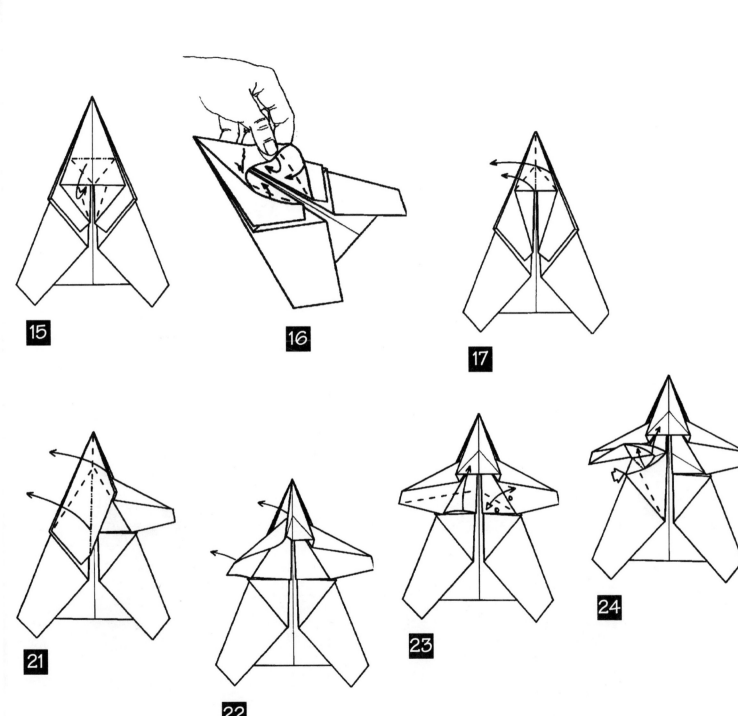

15

16

17

21

22

23

24

get made in the process. The intersection of the creases is the end of that center-pocket-thingy we moved left in the last step. Here is the weird part: It's easier to nail down the creases once you get the layers looking like the next step.

Step 19

You're pulling the layers up and to the right. I like to nail down the marked point first and then move the other stuff into place.

Step 20

Just when you thought it was safe to go to the next step... ha ha ha (maniacal laugh) ... REPEAT FOR THE OTHER SIDE.

Step 21 Do it to it.

Step 22 Here it goes again.

Step 23

O.k. a little more fun than root canal. Some folks like a reference for this fold, so you can fold the marked raw edge to the marked creased edge and unfold. Then use the end of the crease near the center for a reference end point— the corner of the wing is the other end. Crease the TOP LAYER ONLY on the left side.

Step 24

With luck your model looks like this— a⁻ bubble of paper sticking up. This is a compound move coming up here. You're going to squash the point with the big arrow flat while moving the layers marked with the smaller arrows up. Notice the mountain fold indicated. That will happen as a consequence of everything else you're doing.

Ste

Let me just take my glasses off for emphasis here as I congratulate you on the completion of that move. Now back to work. Tuck this flap under here.

Step 26

This step shows the pre-creased reference fold mentioned in step 23. Because now you have to do that whole thing again— to the right side. HA HA HA (louder maniacal laughing). This top layer goes up.

Step 2

This oozy-bob gets twiddled with.

Step 28

And this flap goes under the layer.

Step 29

Fold these two flaps out as shown— corner to corner.

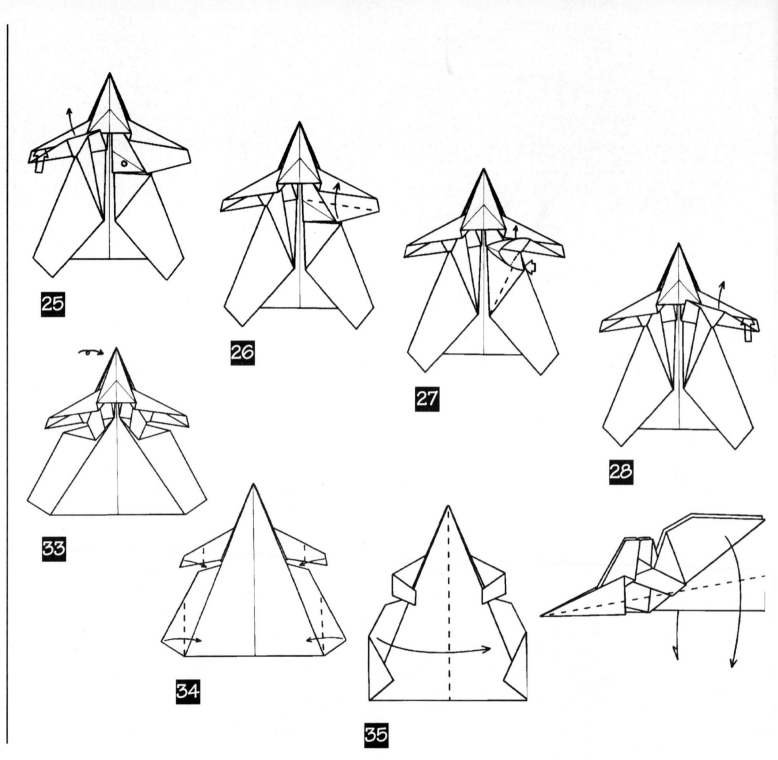

This is almost a direct rip-off of Michael G. LaFosse's F-14 Tomcat. He starts with a square, and his waterbomb base has a shorter back layer. Other than that, Michael, you should be proud of this truly twisted folding procedure. The Super Canard will do giant loops indoors or out. You can't make a more impressive looker that will out fly the competition. Canard, winglet, and standard elevator adjustments will all help make this bird fly the way you desire. There are a lot of control surfaces to tinker with and master.

Step 30 Unfold.

Step 31 Reverse this point.

Step 32

Now reverse the other point.

Step 33

You really deserve a medal for making it this far...or maybe a straight jacket. Basically you're just going to make some winglet folds and wing folds from here. So flip me over and get on with it.

Step 34

You know, Thay is one of those incredible folders who can eye-ball creases down to the gnats petuti, so it doesn't bother him to make winglet creases first. That's the way he drew this plane. Just look at this and know this is where your winglet folds will go.

Step 35

Fold the plane in half.

Step 36

Make the wing folds so that the major creased edge on the other side meets the center line crease of the plane. After making the wing crease is when I like to make winglets. So knock yourself out. They should be parallel with the wing crease. (diagram is not quite right here)

The finished Super Canard.

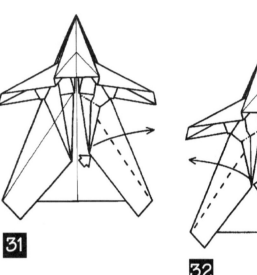

31

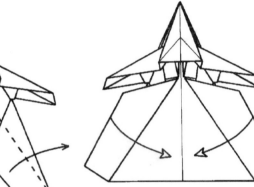

29

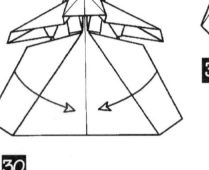

30

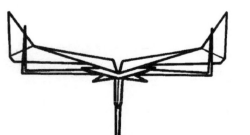

32

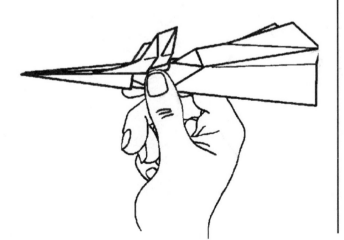

Follow Foils

These are remote control planes requiring no wires, batteries, or radios. With practice, minutes aloft or even an hour is possible. They are very light wing loading, very slow flying speed, and have an ability to be balanced on an updraft of air that you will create.

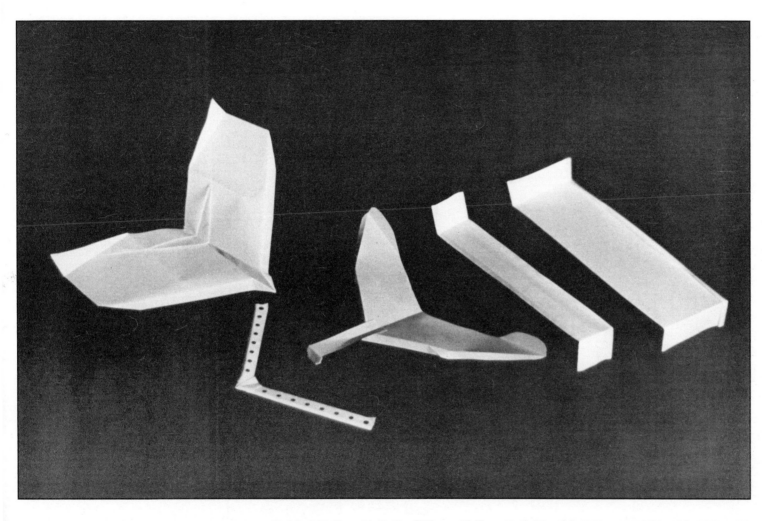

Folded Follow Foil, Perf Plane, Follow Foil, Tumble Wing, and Tumble Wing II.

Tumble Wing

by John M. Collins

Step 1

Start with phone book paper. Fold up about a third. To figure out a third just make the layered part the same size as the unlayered part.

Step 2

Fold the flap in half and unfold.

Step 3

Rip (or if you're a scissor weanie, cut) the page in half.

Step 4

Mountain fold in half and unfold.

Step 5

Fold the lower part in half and unfold.

Step 6

Again fold to the crease and unfold. Also make a mountain fold the same width across the top and unfold. Just eye-ball it in there. Get out of here with that ruler.

Step 7

Fold the ends about an inch in. One gets a mountain and the other gets a valley.

Step 8

The finished Tumble Wing.

The trick is to launch your Tumble Wing into this updraft and keep it there by adjusting both position of the cardboard and your walking speed. Say these words to yourself and believe them: This takes practice. No one does it right the first time. Not even me

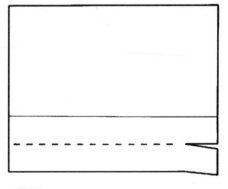

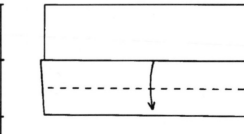

1   **2**   **3**

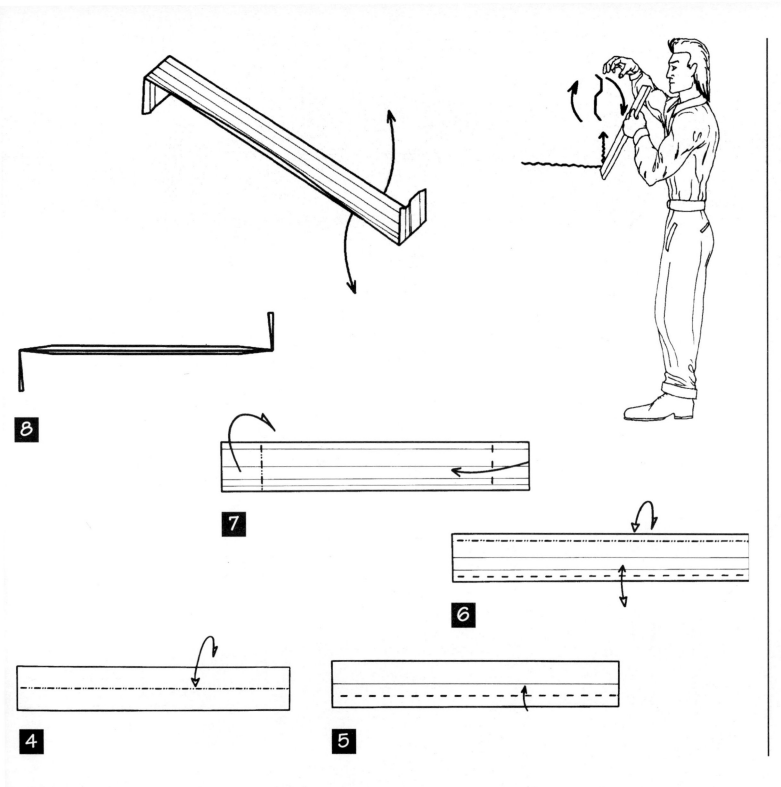

It rotates as shown. The first trick is to get it tumble in a straight line. You can correct turning by adding or subtracting edge droop asymmetrically. In other words try bending one edge up more than the other to add drag. This will slow that side of the wing down. Make sure the fins stay vertical. The reason for the one up, one down configuration is to present maximum resistance to side-slip.

Once it's flying straight, the next trick is to keep it aloft with the cardboard air dam. Hold the cardboard in one hand and walk about the speed the wing travels forward. You should have a fee for the speed after your flight testing. The cardboard should be nearly vertical with the top leaned back only slightly (never lean it back any more than the drawing). Never lean the cardboard forward. If you do, you'll send a current of air toward the floor instead of toward the ceiling.

You see, as you walk forward, air will be forced around the cardboard. If you hold it correctly, the cardboard creates an updraft as you move forward. The trick is to launch your Tumble Wing into this updraft and keep it there by adjusting both position of the cardboard and your walking speed. Say these words to yourself and believe them: *This takes practice. No one does it right the first time. Not even me.*

Eventually, you WILL be able to fly your wing around the house.

Tumble Wing II

by John M. Collins

Step 1

Start with phone book paper. Caution here. Some people hate finding the very page they need is missing from their yellow pages. It's best to find an old phone book. Once you get one, you'll never use it up. Besides, the pages seem to get more crisp with age. Fold the page in half and unfold.

Step 2

Rip (or if you're a scissor weanie, cut) the page in half.

Step 3

Fold the edges as shown. If you're into measuring, it's something like an eighth of an inch.

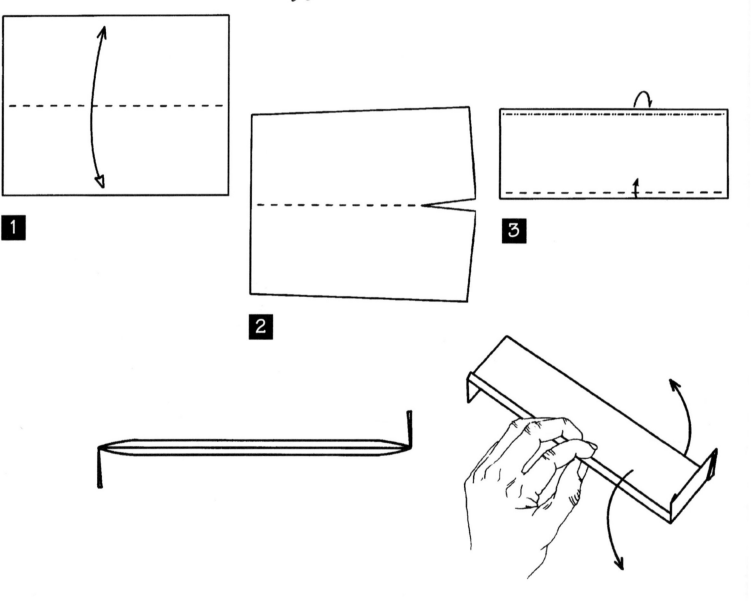

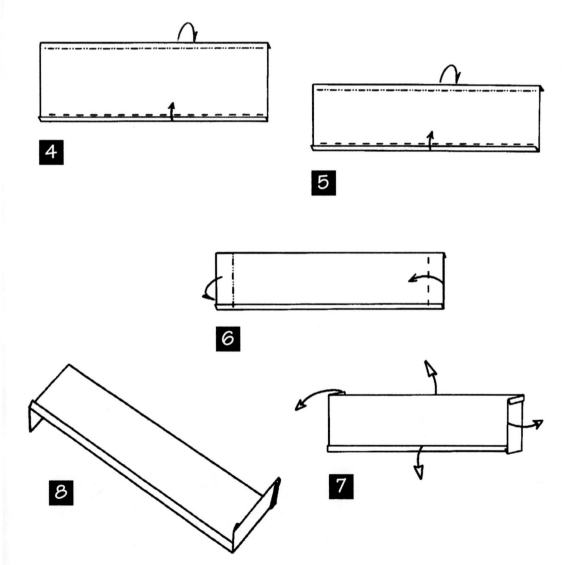

4

5

6

8

7

As you can tell by now, there's no real magic to the width of the paper used to make a tumble wing. I just picked convenient sizes and showed you a couple of wing forms. This one also rotates with the top edge moving toward you as you fly it. As with the other tumble wing, correct turning by adding or subtracting edge droop asymmetrically. In other words try bending on edge up more than the other to add drag. This will slow that side of the wing down.

For flying instructions, refer to the Tumble Wing or Follow Foil.

Step 4

Fold the edges again.

Step 5

And one more time with this edge thing.

Step 6

Fold one end up and one end down.

Step 7

Pull the ends up vertical and also pull the edges open to roughly vertical.

Step 8

The finished Tumble Wing II.

Perf Plane

by John M. Collins

Step 1

Obtain a piece of that computer paper edge stuff that most people just throw away. A chunk that comes off a regular size sheet (11 inches long) works great.

Step 2

Tie it in a knot— being careful to get the knot as close to the center as you can manage.

Step 3

The knot coming together.

Step 4

Just pull it tight... carefully centering as you go.

Step 5

Whoa! Unexpected bonus— you've just learned how to make a perfect pentagon without a pro-

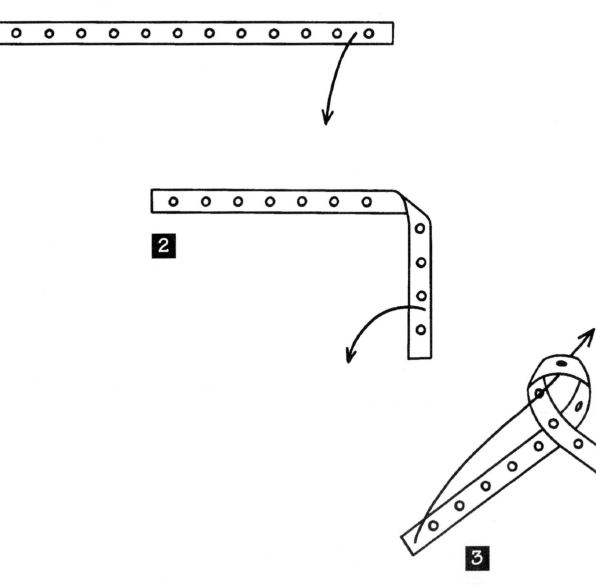

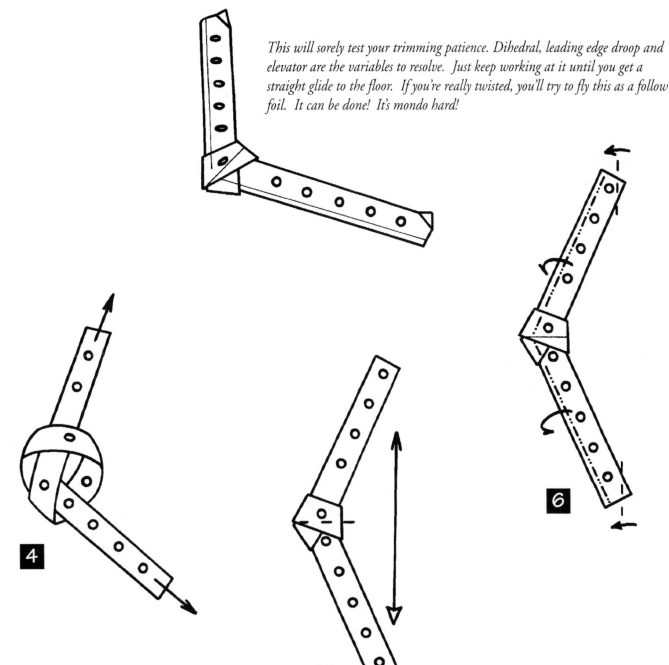

This will sorely test your trimming patience. Dihedral, leading edge droop and elevator are the variables to resolve. Just keep working at it until you get a straight glide to the floor. If you're really twisted, you'll try to fly this as a follow foil. It can be done! It's mondo hard!

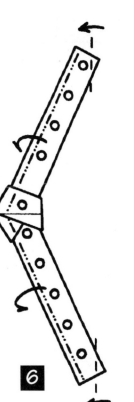

tractor. Give it crease in the center. You might check symmetry during this move and unceremoniously rip or snip off anything sticking out past the short side.

Step 6

Now make tiny leading edge creases. And also tiny up elevator flaps.

The finished Perf Plane. This will sorely test your trimming patience. Dihedral, leading edge droop and elevator are the variables to resolve. Just keep working at it until you get a straight glide to the floor.

If you're really twisted, you'll try to fly this as a follow foil. It can be done! It's mondo hard!

Follow Foil

by John M. Collins

Step 1

Start with phone book paper. Fold it in half (book fold) and then trace the template onto the paper lining up the short straight edge with your crease. Cut (oh geeze I said the word) around the shape. Don't cut the crease. The idea is to create symmetrical wings. Also, you should use the template crease guides as you start making creases in the middle of nowhere on your foil.

Step 2

Make leading edge creases. (view from top of wing)

Step 3

Continue leading edge creases.

Step 4

The upper crease is made by folding in half and unfolding. The lower crease is made by the point to the crease and unfolding.

Step 5

Elevator crease go in right here. The curved dotted lines show where you may have to bend in some down flap. Don't do it yet. The squared off dotted line outlines where you will attach the canard.

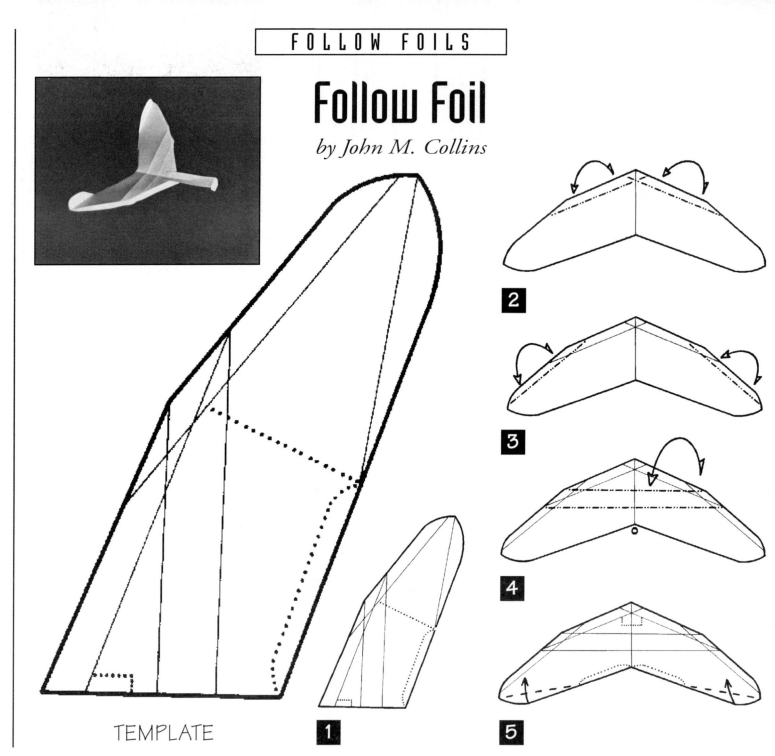

TEMPLATE

1

2

3

4

5

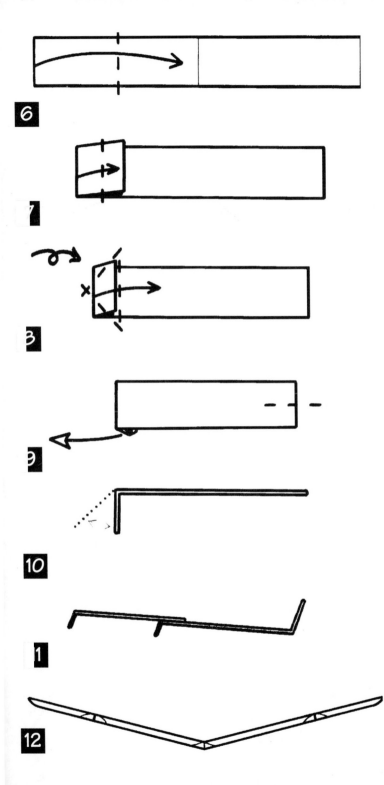

The first trick is to get it flying in a straight line. You can correct turning by adding or subtracting elevator asymmetrically. In other words try bending one flap up more than the other to add drag. This will slow that side of the wing down. You can do the same with the leading edge to a small extent. If the wing is stalling, try adding the down flap where shown in step 6. You can also adjust the angle of the flap on the canard to help get the attitude right.

Once it's flying straight, the next trick is to keep it aloft with the cardboard air dam. Hold the cardboard in one hand and walk about the speed the wing travels forward. You should have a feel for the speed after your flight testing. The cardboard should be nearly vertical with the top leaned back only slightly (never lean it back any more than the drawing). Never lean the cardboard forward. If you do, you'll send a current of air toward the floor instead of toward the ceiling.

You see, as you walk forward, air will be forced around the cardboard. If you hold it correctly, the cardboard creates an updraft as you move forward.

I prefer to place the Follow Foil on one hand, palm up and fingers spread wide open. I put the foil out on the fingers like a hot dog on a grill. Then position the grill over the cardboard and start to walk forward. The updraft should slip right through the grill and lift the foil out of your hand. Ease your hand out of the air stream and grab the other side of the cardboard. You have to adjust position of the cardboard and your walking speed to keep the foil in the updraft. This is not easy.

Say these words to yourself and believe them: *This takes practice. No one does this right the first time. Not even me.*

Eventually, you will be able to fly your foil around the house. Turning is accomplished by moving the cardboard under one wing more than the other causing the wing to bank and turn. This is a very maneuverable wing after you get the hang of it. You'll be circling the coffee table, doing laps around the dining room and blasting down the hallway for speed runs. You have to think of this like a skill sport— skate boarding, golf, tennis,— the more you do it, the better you get. No one starts at the professional level. If you have difficulty learning to fly this one, start with the Tumble Wing. Most people can learn to fly the Tumble Wing easier than the Follow Foil.

Step 6

Cut out a strip 6.25" by .75". Fold this strip in half and unfold. Fold the end to the crease. Then fold again.

Step 7

Fold the layered portion in half one more time.

Step 8

Fold the layered portion in half again.

Step 9

Fold the corners over. Just the tips of the corners. Also, fold along the crease edge. Then flip over.

Step 10

Make a pinch about an inch long in the raw edge end— right in the center. Also open the flap out to about 90 degrees. With a piece of scotch tape, attach the canard. Use a small piece, an inch long at most. The pinch should rest in the center crease of the wing.

Step 11

A profile view of the wing with canard.

Step 12

Dihedral should be like this or a little flatter.

Folded Follow Foil

by John M. Collins

Step 1

Start with phone book paper. Fold the Slo-Mo through step 8.

Step 2

Make a reverse fold, parallel with the leading edge, that starts at the corner shown.

Step 3

Make a wing fold parallel with the main fuselage crease; just above the small triangle you folded back to lock all the layers in place. Also notice that in order to do this, you'll have to squash fold the layers shown with the x-ray view. Take a look at the step 4 diagram before you try this.

Step 4

This is a sort of a petal fold. The main reference point is the valley fold on the top layer. Fold the raw edge of the large triangle to the point—folding the triangle in half. Then make the creases that are partially shown by x-ray view. The mountain fold will happen as you try to flat-

You'll need to use every trick in the book to make this thing work. It's a real test of your trimming and follow foil flying skill. I advise starting with the Tumble Wing or Follow Foil. Then try flying this one. As with other follow foils, get the thing fling straight before you attempt the big trick. You'll have to play with leading edge droop, dihedral angle, elevator adjust, and probably some asymmetrical elevator or leading edge moves to get this one flying. It can be done with patience. The reward is great. A remote control flying machine made from just folding. It represents what John considers to be his ultimate folding achievement.

ten this step. Don't flatten the center crease of the large triangle after you make the mountain folds. You'll deal with that in step 5.

Step 5

Now you can flatten that little flap by first folding down then up. Make the mountain folds in the wings by folding parallel with the main wing fold and through the corners shown. Then make the other main wing crease.

Step 6

Spread the wing and rest the plane with the fuselage up.

Bend the wing sharply where shown with the valley fold marks. The bend should be parallel with the leading edge. The nose of the plane gets pinched together after the bends are complete. Make the elevator folds at right angles to the raw edges of the wing tips. The crease should end at the mid wing crease. The finished Folded Follow Foil.

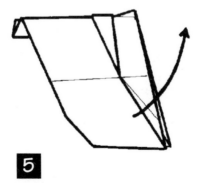

5

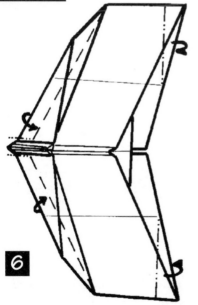

6

History

1. Early publications on the subject mentioned in The Great International Paper Airplane Book (vide infra) are (1) H.G.G.Herklots, Paper Aeroplanes (an essay), W.Heffer & Sons Ltd, Cambridge, England,1931; (2) Richard Katz, Das Kleine Buch vom Papierflugzeug, 1933; and (3) Pawel Elsztein, Duza Ksiazka o Malych Samolatach, Nasza Ksiergarnia, Warsaw, Poland, 1956.

2. J.Mander, G.Dipple and H.Gossage, The Great International Paper Book, Simon and Schuster, New York, 1967.

3. The waterbomb is an origami base fold that finds extensive use in glider construction and will be discussed in detail in the chapter on folding basics. particularly striking origami glider by J.M.Sakoda, folded from a square, had a long needle nose and a diamond shaped wing. In all, there were nearly 12,000 entrants from 28 different countries in the First International Paper Airplane Contest!

4. R.S.Barnaby, How to Make & Fly Paper Airplanes, Four Winds Press, New York, 1968.

5. E.Nakamura, Flying Origami: Origami from Pure Fun to True Science, Japan Publications, Inc. (through Harper & Row), New York , 1972.

6. Cambering is curving a wing surface. The camber of a wing is the amount the wing arches above a straight line connecting the leading and trailing edges of the wing. The leading edge of a wing is the forward or front edge that meets the wind. The trailing edge is its aft or rear edge. The terms leading edge and trailing edge also apply to fins.

A big vacuum exists in regard to the early history of paper gliders. There is little information on what was known and practiced before this century. Of course, paper gliders cannot have been very common before paper became cheaply and widely available, which might set a starting date.[] Who it was that first folded a sheet of paper into the classic schoolroom dart, known now all around the world by almost every school child, will never be known. Perhaps the first improvements on the simple dart were made when paper became a disposable commodity in the school room.

Clearly, there is likely to have been development of the paper glider paralleling and coming out of the growing art of paper folding in the early days of origami. The fact that a piece of paper could be folded in some intricate way into the shape of a bird which would glide when tossed into the air did not escape notice. The folded form was more than a model; it could function as a plane!

Recent history of the folded paper glider is revealed by the literature. From the 1930's and on[1], books provide a trail of the steady advances being made in the art. There are several pivotal or landmark events. The promotional campaign waged by the magazine Scientific American for an international competition and the resultant compendium The Great International Paper Airplane Book[2] awakened the world to the extensive interest in and contemporary importance of the paper glider. The world was newly engaged in space exploration. Drawings for a supersonic transport were on many drawing boards. It was an age of unprecedented powerful aerospace machines and enthusiasm for them.

Origami (folded) gliders were the order of the day in The Great International Paper Airplane Book. Besides simple rectangular flying wings and standard darts, quite a few gliders featured nose locks or other fairly sophisticated origami constructions (like spike noses). The waterbomb[3] fold was in evidence, too.

One of the winners of the First International Paper Airplane Contest (aerobatics/professional class) was R.S.Barnaby. A year or so later (1968) How to Make & Fly Paper Airplanes by Barnaby appeared[4]. While this book did not offer any new folding, it did deal in considerable depth with the aerodynamics and the practical practice of paper glider flying. There was more to flying a paper glider than just giving it a toss!

A few years were to pass before new impetus was given to the origami side of paper gliders. Published in 1972, Flying Origami by E.Nakamura revealed new potential in the folding method of paper glider construction[5]. Nakamura applied traditional origami techniques to create gliders of new shapes. A simple nose fold locking technique appeared in print in an English publication for the first time. Stiffening and cambering[6] folds were used along the leading edge of some wings for the first time, too. Nakamura also innovated on the theme of two piece gliders where wings and fuselages are separate folded pieces. He went beyond strictly folding, however. Many of his gliders had cuts made to facilitate folding a novel shape (kirigami). Also, many of his gliders employed staples and glue for fastening and laminating.

Evidently a considerable time was needed for all of this to

become digested by other people. In 1981 H.R.Bergan published his The Lingore Paper Airplane Folding Manual[7]. Bergan's work built systematically and methodically upon the base established by The Great International Paper Airplane Book and Flying Origami. He recognized the first generalization of the waterbomb, which he called a variable angle pocket fold. He also invented a new locking method for rectangular wings. He carried the use of kirigami to construct wings and realistic fuselages to an extreme. Perhaps his key contribution was a meticulous and extensive exploration of the two piece glider.

Meanwhile the pure origami glider was alive and well in Australia in the hands of C.Morris. His book The Best Paper Aircraft became available in the United States in the mid 1980's[8]. It showed the continued vitality and viability of the strict folding approach by exhibiting a variety of new glider models or novel variations on older themes. A contemporaneous and comparable contribution from the United States was Wings & Things by S.Weiss[9]. Like Nakamura's Flying Origami Weiss's book is a mixture of flying models of creatures and planes and a variety of other flying things. Another book of this sort is Paper Flight by Dutch puzzle expert J. Botermans[10].

Development of glider controls was not being neglected either. A seminal but at the time (1985) little recognized contribution was the "slat" of P.Vollheim[11]. The "slat" is an angled crease made near the leading edge of a wing paralleling the leading edge or sometimes running further from it at the wingtip. The "slat" has a variety of control uses and can impart stability to a glider tending to instability.

Vollheim's folded gliders[11,12,13] generally involve only the simplest of folding techniques. Tape fastens loose folds down. A fair amount of cutting (including cut-in fins and flaps) is used. Paper clips are applied to weight the nose. Materials other than paper (such as card stock and plastic straws) are used for many of his gliders. The absence of folding innovations is compensated by a keen sense for glider esthetics and function and contributions in the area of control systems.

The sport of hang gliding inspired some paper glider experts. A new flying wing fold (by cutting, folding and stapling) and further understanding of paper glider aerodynamics were offered by E.Hui in Amazing Paper Airplanes[14].

But in the interim a significant event had transpired that seemed to portend negatively for the folded paper glider. This was the Second Great International Paper Airplane Contest sponsored jointly by Science 86 magazine, Seattle's Museum of Flight, and the Smithsonian Institution's National Air and Space Museum and held in Seattle, Washington in May 1985. The contest is documented in THE Paper Airplane Book[15]. Except for a few standard folded designs and what appears[16] to be a novel folded flying wing (by G.C.Fisher), all categories were dominated by laminated gliders cut out of card stock and glued up. Most winning gliders were of the conventional airplane configuration with a tail section on a fuselage behind a main wing[17] of laminated construction[18]. But where were the origami innovations that one would have thought would have been inspired in large numbers by the works of Nakamura, Bergan, Morris, Weiss and others? There was not

7. H.R.Bergan, The Lingore Paper Airplane Folding Manual, Charles E. Tuttle Co., Rutland, VT (originally published by Lingore Press, Potsdam, NY), 1981. Bergan fastens with staples (but eschews glue) and ballasts with paper clips. He prefers both these because they allow repositioning and adjustment.

8. C.Morris, The Best Paper Aircraft, Perigree Books, The Putnam Publishing Co., New York, 1983, 1984. This was followed in 1988 by the appearance of More Best Paper Aircraft.

9. S.Weiss, Wings & Things: Origami That Flies St. Martin's Press, New York, 1984.

10. J.Botermans, Paper Flight, Henry Holt and Co., New York, 1983.

11. P.Vollheim, 30 Planes for the Paper Pilot, Pocket Books, (Simon & Schuster), New York, 1985.

12. P.Vollheim, The Paper Ace, Contemporary Books, Inc., New York, 1987.

13. P.Vollheim, 30 More Planes for the Paper Pilot, Pocket Books, (Simon & Schuster), New York, 1988.

14. E.Hui, Amazing Paper Airplanes, St. Martin's Press, New York, 1988.

15. A.L.Hammond and A.Fujino, eds., THE Paper Airplane Book: ThE Official Book of the Second Great International Paper Airplane Contest, Vintage Books, New York, 1985.

16. Plans for this innovation were omitted from the book.

17. Most folded gliders are of the delta wing sort; the control surfaces are integrated into the main wing and there is no separate tail section.

18. One exception to this was the javelin-like device "Paper Pussycat" of R.B.Meuser that took first place in the non-professional distance category. Meuser had also won in the distance category with a long, narrow folded dart in the First Great International contest of 1967. But the "Paper Pussycat" involved very little folding; it was a cut and glue construction, too.

19. J.M.Collins, The Gliding Flight, Ten Speed Press, Berkeley, CA, 1989.

even a category for origami gliders as in the first contest!

It was a dark day for the origami glider. It looked to some that the glorious days of the elegant but simply folded paper glider were over!

But folding is just too creatively pregnant with possibilities. And it is a rapid and clean construction method. The fact that everything can be constructed from a single unviolated sheet is not a real limitation but a challenge that is a continuing source of non-conventional ideas.

The origami glider was raised from the ashes in new splendor by J.M.Collins a few years later in The Gliding Flight19. This book inspires with numerous new origami, all strictly folded from a sheet of notepaper. No cuts are made, no tape is used, no glues are applied, no staples are punched in and no paper clips encumber the form!

The present book builds from this point in the history of the origami glider. These gliders continue to get better and better yet.

About the Authors

John M. Collins

John M. Collins is married to Suzanne Collins and has a son Sean. John is television director for KRON TV in San Francisco, CA. He wrote "The Gliding Flight" (Ten Speed Press 1989). John has taught paper folding for the San Francisco and Marin County library systems as well as the annual international origami convention in New York (sponsored by The Friends of the Origami Center, NYC).

John has appeared on television flying paper planes for "The Morning Show", CBS; "Next Step", The Discovery Channel; "Seattle Today", KING TV; "Sports Final" and "NewsCenter 4", KRON TV. He is also a staff announcer for KRON.

In addition to writing paper airplane books, John has received a "Story By" credit for an episode of the Fox TV series M.A.N.T.I.S.. He also wrote and voiced the script for the new CD ROM "Paper Planes", distributed by WordPerfect/Mainstreet.

Sport kites and boomerangs are among his other interests.

Donald C. Garwood, Ph.D.

Don is a scientist and a very successful inventer. He holds a basic patent (assigned to 3M) that has revolutionized the way orthopedic casts are made and applied. But among his fondest inventions are the many new paper gliders he has created over the past ten years or more.

While working in the aerospace industry in the early years of space exploration, Don was deeply involved in planning scientific missions to explore the planets. Part of many such missions is to get scientific payloads down through a planetary atmosphere to the surface. As a result, he became familiar with the aerodynamics of atmospheric re-entry.

Don is an author of another instruction book: "Masters of Instrumental Blues Guitar" (Oak Publications, 1967) that teaches blues guitar.

Thay Yang

Thay Yang lives in Banning, California. He is the author of two other volumes of paper airplanes: "Exotic Paper Airplanes" and "Exquisite Paper Airplanes" both published by QED Press, Fort Bragg, CA. Thay wrote and illustrated both of those two books, as well as illustrating "Return to the Fold."

Thay placed second in the Senior Aesthetics division for the 1991 Great International Paper Airplane Contest, sponsored by the Seattle Museum of Flight.

"This book is a collaboration between three people who really enjoy (read that obsess about) creating and flying paper airplanes. New paper glider designs, new folding techniques, as well as some novel launching and flying techniques are all explained in easy details. All you need to start is a piece of paper."